Knit&Crochet Combined

BEST OF BOTH WORLDS

Knit&Crochet Combined

BEST OF BOTH WORLDS

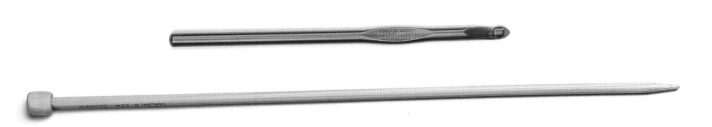

Monette Lassiter Satterfield

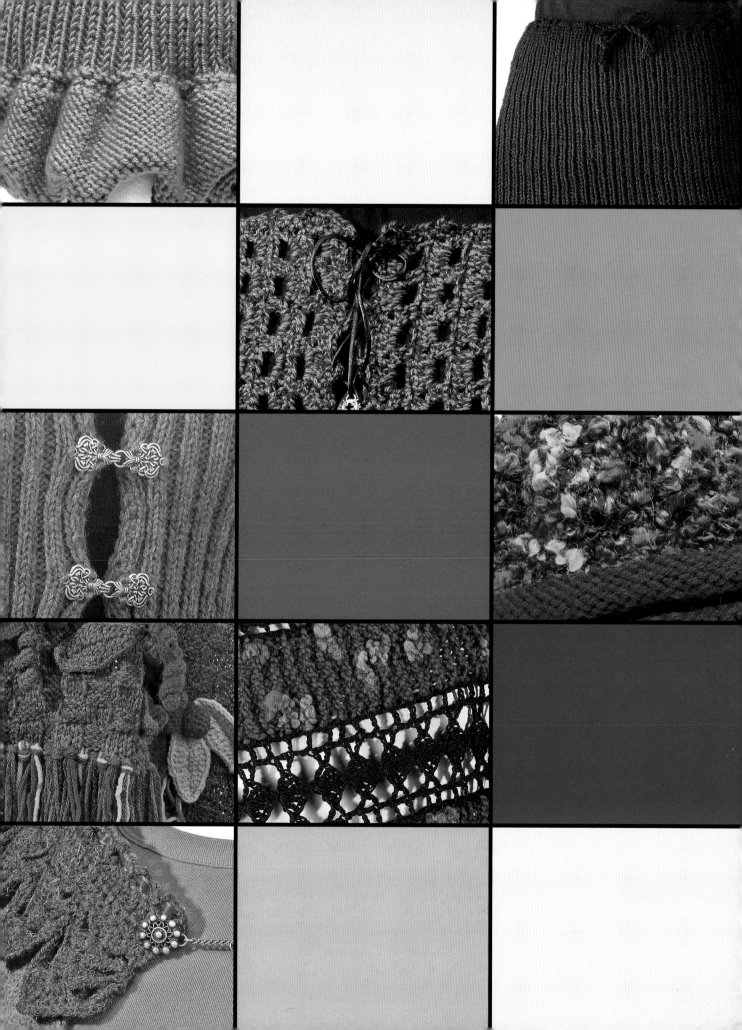

Knit & Crochet Combined

Why the Best of Both Worlds?

I love both knitting and crocheting. Each technique has wonderful characteristics, and the resulting fabrics can be very complementary. When you are brave enough to combine the techniques, a wide range of possibilities opens to you.

One technique is not inherently more difficult than the other; it seems to be more a matter of which you learned first. In my case, I learned to crochet when I was about 12, and didn't learn to knit until another decade had passed. I was fascinated with my new knitting skills, and put down my crochet hooks for several years to focus on knitting. However, a chance crochet project reminded me how much I'd enjoyed crocheting – and how well-suited (in some cases, more so than knitting) it was for certain applications. Now, I enjoy experimenting with both techniques, using them to complement each other.

If you do have a strong preference for one technique, stick with what you love – but remember to venture into the other when it suits your purpose.

Knit

A knitter forms a fabric by making a series of interlocking loops from a continuous yarn using two or more knitting needles. Each loop, or stitch, is formed when a loop of yarn is pulled through an existing stitch already on the needle. A row, or horizontal series of loops, is linked to the row below and above, and each loop on the row is connected to its neighbor to the side. These interconnections give knitted

fabric its characteristic elasticity. It also means that the fabric will ravel if cut unless special precautions are taken. Knit fabric is usually stockinette stitch, or a pattern stitch made up of the two stitches that comprise knitting – knit and purl. While the stitches are simple, they can be put together in numerous ways – from knit/purl brocade patterns to cables to lace.

Compared to crocheted fabric, the structure of basic stockinette stitch produces a supple fabric that drapes well. The surface is smooth and the overall fabric is light. This is, in part, due to the smaller amount of yarn consumed by the stitches. As well as being lighter and more supple, the knitted fabric is generally more elastic, especially lengthwise, than a similar crocheted fabric. This elasticity owes to the basic structure of knitting versus crocheting. The structure of knitting also limits the knitter somewhat in direction changes and shaping and color changes, as there are usually several stitches to contend with on the needles.

Knitted fabric is a good choice in a close-fitting garment (especially in areas like the underarm) where bulk is unwanted. If a garment relies on a more supple and drapable fabric for its appeal, knitting will likely produce a more flattering look, particularly if soft ruffles or A-line shaping are used. A smooth fabric in stockinette stitch also is a good choice for an area you do not wish to call attention to.

The elasticity of ribbing, another popular knit stitch, is an excellent aid to a flattering and comfortable fit.

Crochet

A crocheter begins by placing a slip knot on a hook. Then, another loop is pulled through the first; this is repeated as desired to form a chain. Other stitches are then worked in a similar manner, either by pulling another loop through the chain or by wrapping the yarn around the hook before pulling a loop through the chain and the yarn looped around the hook. In contrast to knitting, with its interdependent loops, each crochet stitch stands on its own and only one loop is in use at a time. This structure contributes to crocheted fabric requiring somewhat more yarn than a knitted fabric, as well as being thicker and less pliant.

Crochet fabric can be made of quite a few more stitches than knitting. Basic stitches include single, double, and treble crochet, as well as numerous variations on these. Not to worry though – the stitches all build on the same basic principle of pulling one loop through another.

When these stitches and their variations are combined, the resulting fabric can be quite a bit more elaborate than a comparable knitted fabric. Crocheted pieces are often thicker and sturdier, due to the larger amount of yarn used in their construction. One of the biggest advantages (or drawbacks, depending on your viewpoint) to crocheted textiles is that they are often much more textured and have greater surface interest than their knitted cousins. This texture includes lace as well. Crochet is admirably suited to making a lovely lace fabric.

Many people, myself included, find that most crochet projects proceed faster than a similar knitting project.

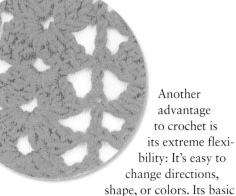

Another advantage to crochet is its extreme flexibility: It's easy to change directions, shape, or colors. Its basic structure allows practically instantaneous changes, as there is only one stitch to contend with at a given time.

Crocheted fabrics lend themselves very well to accent areas such as edgings and collars when worked in decorative stitches and patterns. Crochet is an excellent stabilizing influence on knitted edges that want to curl, stretch, or otherwise misbehave. A decorative pattern or lace stitch for part of a garment will create design interest in what is otherwise a simple pattern. Crochet also works well to create unusual or complicated shapes because it is easy to shape. When warmth is the goal, crocheted fabric, especially in a lofty yarn, provides a bulkier, warmer fabric.

Knit & Crochet combined

The projects in this book were designed to showcase the best characteristics of knitting and crocheting, without being too difficult in either craft. Most are well within the reach of the adventurous beginner. However, a couple are suitable for an intermediate. Be sure to read the directions completely before beginning a project.

If you need more guidance, check the pattern abbreviations (knitting is on page 10 and crocheting is on page 11). The Basics section, beginning on page 74, provides more detail, including step-by-step instructions for most techniques. Stitch illustrations accompany most projects, as well.

Stitch spotlight

These larger photographs show more detail, and give you a closer look at the stitches that comprise the work. Be sure to check Basics for step-by-step instructions for common knit and crochet stitches.

Creative options

At the end of each project, you'll find creative options – suggestions for making the pattern differently from the instructions. I often look at a finished design and try to think of what else could be done to make it a little different or special. This is my way of sharing those ideas with you. There are many ways to customize a pattern and make it your own – these are just a starting point.

Tips

You'll find some tips scattered throughout the book. There are many things to think about and learn, from selecting your yarn to caring for your final garment. It's my way of helping you navigate your journey through the wonderful combined world of knit and crochet.

– Monette Lassiter Satterfield

Commonly Used Knitting Abbreviations

[ ]: work instructions within brackets as many times as directed

( ): work instructions within parentheses in the place directed

*: repeat instructions following the single asterisk as directed

* *: repeat instructions between asterisks as many times as directed or repeat from a given set of instructions

†: repeat instructions following the cross as directed

": inch(es)

alt: alternate

approx: approximately

beg: begin/beginning

bet: between

BO: bind off

CA: color A

CB: color B

CC: contrasting color

cm: centimeter(s)

cn: cable needle

CO: cast on

cont: continue

dec: decrease/decreases/decreasing

dpn: double pointed needle(s)

fl: front loop(s)

foll: follow/follows/following

g: gram(s)

inc: increase/increases/increasing

k or K: knit

k2tog: knit two stitches together

kwise: knitwise

LH: left hand

lp(s): loop(s)

m: meter(s)

mm: millimeter(s)

M1: make one stitch

M1 p-st: make one purl stitch

MC: main color

oz: ounce(s)

p or P: purl

p2tog: purl two stitches together

pat(s) or patt: pattern(s)

pm: place marker

pop: popcorn

prev: previous

psso: pass slipped stitch(es) over

pwise: purlwise

RH: right hand

RS: right side

rem: remain(s)/remaining

rep: repeat(s)

rev St st: reverse stockinette stitch

rnd(s): round(s)

sk: skip

SKP: slip, knit, pass stitch over – one stitch decreased

sk2p: slip one, knit two together, pass slip stitch over the knit two together; two stitches decreased

sl: slip

sl1k: slip one knitwise

sl1p: slip one purlwise

sl st: slip stitch(es)

ss: slip stitch (UK)

ssk: slip, slip, knit two stitches together – a decrease

sssk: slip, slip, slip, knit three stitches together – a decrease

st(s): stitch(es)

St st: stockinette stitch/stocking stitch

tbl: through back loop

tog: together

WS: wrong side

wyib: with yarn in back

wyif: with yarn in front

yd(s): yard(s)

yfwd: yarn forward

yo: yarn over

yon: yarn over needle (UK)

yrn: yarn around needle (UK)

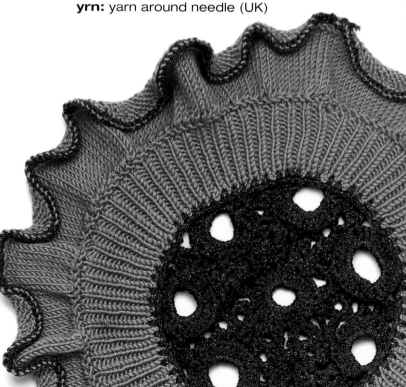

Commonly Used Crocheting Abbreviations

[ ]: work instructions within brackets as many times as directed

( ): work instructions within parentheses in the place directed

*: repeat the instructions following the single asterisk as directed

* *: repeat instructions between asterisks as many times as directed or repeat from a given set of instructions

†: repeat instructions following the cross as directed

": inch(es)

alt: alternate

approx: approximately

beg: begin/beginning

bet: between

BL: back loop(s)

bo: bobble

BP: back post

BPdc: back post double crochet

BPsc: back post single crochet

BPtr: back post treble crochet

CA: color A

CB: color B

CC: contrasting color

ch: chain stitch

ch-: refers to chain or space previously made: e.g., ch-1 space

ch-sp: chain space

CL: cluster

cm: centimeter(s)

cont: continue

dc: double crochet

dc2tog: double crochet two stitches together

dec: decrease/decreases/decreasing

dtr: double treble

FL: front loop(s)

foll: follow/follows/following

FP: front post

FPdc: front post double crochet

FPsc: front post single crochet

FPtr: front post treble crochet

g: gram

hdc: half double crochet

inc: increase/increases/increasing

lp(s): loops

m: meter(s)

MC: main color

mm: millimeter(s)

oz: ounce(s)

p: picot

pat(s) or patt: pattern(s)

pc: popcorn

pm: place marker

prev: previous

rem: remain/remaining

rep: repeat(s)

rnd(s): round(s)

RS: right side

sc: single crochet

sc2tog: single crochet two stitches together

sk: skip

Sl st: slip stitch

sp(s): space(s)

st(s): stitch(es)

tch or t-ch: turning chain

tbl: through back loop

tog: together

tr: treble crochet

trtr: triple treble crochet

WS: wrong side

yd(s): yard(s)

yo: yarn over

yoh: yarn over hook

Projects

Toasty topper

Add this warm, colorful hat to your winter wardrobe

Simple yet nontraditional stitches give this hat a striking texture and a comfortable fit. The band, knitted flat and seamed at the back, is worked in a horizontal rib made of alternating stockinette and reverse stockinette rows. Also known as Quaker Rib, this pattern stretches easily, making it ideal for a hat.

The crown is crocheted in the round with a colorful bouclé yarn. Pairing highly textured yarn with simple crochet stitches creates the stiffness that keeps the top from collapsing. Increases and decreases give the crown its striking shape.

To complete the hat, knit an I-cord with the main yarn, coil it, and attach it to the center of the crown.

Sizing
Finished size: To fit adult size medium, approximately 21-22 in. (53-56cm) in circumference

Gauge
Knit: 16 stitches/4 in. (10cm) in stockinette stitch
Crochet: 2 stitches/1 in. (2.5cm) in single crochet

Materials
- skein worsted-weight yarn, main color (Wool-Ease, Lion Brand Yarn Company, Purple #147)
- skein bouclé yarn, accent color (Lion Bouclé, Lion Brand, Tutti Fruitti #930)
- knitting needles, size 8 (5mm) or size needed to obtain gauge
- double-pointed knitting needles, size 8 (5mm)
- crochet hook, size N or size needed to obtain gauge
- tapestry or yarn needle
- tape measure
- yarn cutter

Reverse stockinette and stockinette stitch combine to make substantial horizontal ribbing.

Knit the hat band

1 With knitting needles and MC yarn, CO 88 stitches.

2 Work six rows reverse stockinette stitch. (Purl the first row, knit the second row, then keep in pattern.)

3 Work six rows stockinette stitch. (Knit the first row, purl the second row, then keep in pattern.)

4 Repeat steps 2–3 once.

5 Work six rows reverse stockinette. You will have five pattern bands. BO and work in ends.

6 Sew the short ends of the band together.

Crochet the crown

Note: Ch 1 at the beginning of each round.

1 With accent color yarn and crochet hook, attach yarn to right side of band. (The right side has three rows of reverse stockinette stitch facing.)

2 Ch 1, sc in every other knit stitch around (44 stitches). Join to beginning ch 1 with slip stitch.

3 Work two rounds even in sc.

4 Work increase round by making 2 sc in each stitch around (88 stitches).

5 Work one round even.

6 Work decrease round by working 2 sc together around (44 stitches).

7 Work second decrease round (22 stitches).

8 Work three rounds even.

9 Work decrease round (11 stitches).

10 Work last decrease round (6 stitches).

Fasten off and use tail of yarn to draw remaining opening closed. Work in ends.

Knit an I-cord

1 With double-pointed needles, CO 5 stitches MC yarn and k to end.

2 Slide to other end of double-pointed needle. Pull yarn snug, k to end. Repeat until cord is 22 in. (56cm) long. Cut yarn, thread tail through all stitches, and secure. Work in ends.

3 Coil I-cord and sew it to the top of the hat.

CREATIVE OPTIONS

Instead of the coiled I-cord, attach a giant pom-pom to the crown.

Make small tassels and hang them around the bottom of the crown so they drape over the ribbed band.

Attach large colorful beads or sequins randomly on the crown.

"Lofty" yarns —
Loft refers to the amount
of air trapped inside a
yarn between the fibers
themselves and the strands
that form the yarn.
Garments made of high-loft
yarn tend to be warm and
hold their shape well.

Crochet the scarf

1 With accent yarn and crochet hook, ch 16.

Row 1: Hdc in 4th ch from hook, * ch 1, skip 1 ch, hdc in next ch, repeat from * across, ch 3, turn (7 ch 1 spaces).

Row 2: *Skip ch 1 space in previous row, hdc in previous hdc, ch 1, repeat from * across, ending with hdc in turning ch, ch 3, turn.

2 Repeat row 2 until scarf is desired length, omit turning ch 3 and BO.

Knit the scarf edging

1 With main yarn and knitting needles, pick up 28 stitches along short edge of scarf.

2 Work eight rows reverse stockinette stitch. (Purl the first row, knit the second row, then keep in pattern.)
Work eight rows stockinette stitch. (Knit the first row, purl the second row, then keep in pattern.)

3 Repeat previous 16 rows once. Work eight rows reverse stockinette. You will have five pattern bands.

4 BO and work in ends.

CREATIVE OPTIONS

Make yourself a coordinating rib-trimmed scarf to complete your ensemble. Buy another ball of the accent yarn to finish this additional project.

Cute cap

Pair a striking crocheted centerpiece with a flirty knit ruffle for a charming cap

This soft, lightweight cap features a lacy crocheted crown, worked in a glittery yarn. The sides are knit in the round in k 1, p 1 ribbing, ending with a stockinette stitch ruffle. To knit the ruffle, you'll eventually be increasing to 480 stitches. This many stitches can be challenging to work, but knitting in the round eliminates having to purl back across the stitches, so the piece is easier to handle. The bind-off row is worked in the glittery yarn, unifying the two pieces.

Make a matching bag (see Creative Options, p. 21) by crocheting one crown motif and attaching it to the front of a small crocheted bag.

Sizing
Finished size: To fit adult size medium, approximately 20 in. (51cm) circumference

Gauge
Knit: 24 stitches/4 in. (10cm) in k 1, p 1 ribbing
Crochet: One motif is 8 in. (20cm) in diameter at the widest part worked with smaller hook.

Materials
- skein medium-weight yarn, main color (Glitterspun, Lion Brand Yarn Company, Amethyst #144)
- **2** skeins double-knit, lightweight, or light worsted yarn, accent color (Microspun, Lion Brand, Lavender #143)
- crochet hooks, sizes G-6 (4mm) and H-8 (5mm) or size needed to obtain gauge
- 16-in. (41cm) circular knitting needles, size 4 (3.5mm) or size needed to obtain gauge
- tapestry or yarn needle
- tape measure
- pins
- yarn cutter

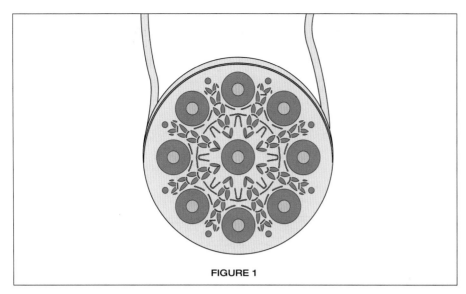

FIGURE 1

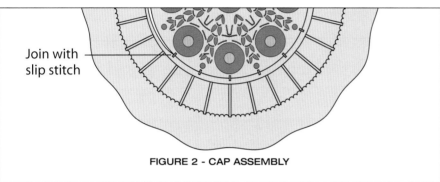

Join with slip stitch

FIGURE 2 - CAP ASSEMBLY

FIGURE 3 - MOTIF STITCH DIAGRAM

Crown motif

With smaller hook, ch 8 MC yarn, join with slip stitch to form ring.

Round 1: Ch 3 (counts as 1 dc), 31 dc into ring, sl st to top of ch 3 (32 stitches).

Round 2: Ch 3, 1 dc into same place as ch 3 (counts as dc2tog or "cluster"), ch 3, work dc2tog into same place as last cluster, * ch 7, skip 3 stitches, work (dc2tog, ch 3, dc2tog) into next ch 3 space; repeat from * six more times, ch 7, skip 3 stitches, sl st to top of first cluster (7 ch 7 loops).

Round 3: Sl st into next ch, ch 3, 1 dc in same place as ch 3 (counts as dc2tog or cluster), ch 3, work dc2tog into same ch 3 space, *ch 7, skip 7 ch, work (dc2tog, ch 3, dc2tog) into next ch 3 space; repeat from * six more times, ch 7, skip 7 ch, sl to top of first cluster.

Round 4: Sl st into next ch, ch 3, 1 dc in same place as ch 3 (counts as dc2tog or cluster), ch 3, work dc2tog into same ch 3 space, *ch 4, 1 sc under 7 ch arch of 2nd round so as to enclose 7 ch arch of 3rd round, ch 4**, work (dc2tog, ch 3, dc2tog) into next ch 3 space; repeat from * six more times and from * to ** again, sl to top of first cluster.

Round 5: Sl st into next ch, ch 3, 1 dc in same place as ch 3 (counts as dc2tog or cluster), ch 3, work dc2tog into same ch 3 space, * ch 15, sl st into 12th chain from hook, ch 3, sl st to top of cluster just made, 6 dc into 12 ch ring, skip 4 ch, sl st to next sc, 8 dc into ring, skip 4 ch (inner half of border circle completed) **, work (dc2tog, 3ch, dc2tog) into next ch 3 space; repeat from * six more times and from * to ** again, sl to top of first cluster.

Round 6: *Ch 1, work (dc2tog, 6ch, sl st to 5th chain from hook, ch 1 dc2tog) into next ch 3 space, 1 ch, sl st to top of next cluster, 16 dc into 12 chain ring (outer half of border circle completed), sl st to top of next cluster; repeat from * seven times. Fasten off. (See Figure 3.)

Crochet the crown

With smaller crochet hook and MC yarn, make one motif as directed. Work in ends.

Knit the band

1 With knitting needles and accent yarn, CO 144 stitches, join, and begin working in the round.

2 Work in k 1, p 1 ribbing for 2 in. (5cm).

3 K one round (becomes right side of band), p one round.

4 Work bar increase round: K in front and back of each stitch around (288 stitches).

5 Continue in stockinette stitch until ruffle measures 2 in. (5cm).

6 P one round.

7 Work increase round: K1, inc 1 around as before (480 stitches).

8 Cut accent yarn and attach main yarn. BO all stitches purlwise. Work in ends.

Assemble the cap

1 Pin crown to band at ch 5 picots and middle of border circles. Adjust band to fit evenly.

2 With larger crochet hook and MC yarn, attach yarn to cast on edge of band. Ch 1, work 1 sc in every other stitch around (in each knit stitch facing) attaching band to crown at picot points and middle of border circles with slip stitches. Work around to start and join with slip stitch. Fasten off and work in ends. (See Figure 2.)

STITCH SPOTLIGHT

The ruffled edge is formed by the dramatic increase made in the last round of stitches.

CREATIVE OPTIONS

Choose your own sparkly color scheme. The main yarn could be gold or silver with white or black; or perhaps ruby with cherry red.

The band of this hat is ripe for embellishment. Try buttons of any type – large and colorful or small and shiny.

Sew seed beads around the edge of the ruffle to add even more sparkle.

Or, make a matching bag (see Figure 1):

With MC yarn and smaller hook, make crown motif, work in ends, and set aside.

1 With accent yarn and smaller hook, ch 2.

Round 1: 6 sc in second ch from hook. Sl st in first sc.

Round 2: 1 ch, 2 sc in each sc around. Sl st in first sc (12 sc).

Round 3: 1 ch, (1 sc in next sc, 2 sc in next sc) around. Sl st in first sc (18 sc).

Round 4: 1 ch, (1 sc in each of next 2 sc, 2 sc in next sc) around. Sl st in first sc (24 sc).

Following rounds: For each new round, add 1 extra sc stitch to the number of sc stitches between increases. For example, round 5 would have 3 sc between increases, then round 6 would have 4 sc between increases, and so on.

2 Continue until piece measures slightly larger than crown motif. Fasten off. Repeat to make a second piece.

3 Holding two sc rounds together, sc around through both thicknesses, leaving the top one third unworked for bag opening. Attach crown motif to one side of bag.

4 Chain desired length for strap and work one to five rows of sc across, as desired. Fasten off and work in all ends.

Stunning stole

Blend two strikingly different yarns to create a memorable stole with a beautiful drape

Care in yarn selection – and stitches that complement the selected yarns – combine to make this design stand out. For the knit sections, use a yarn with plenty of texture and color interest, like this thick yarn with multicolored slubs. This yarn is well-suited to a simple stitch that drapes well, like garter stitch. For the crochet sections, a plain, smooth yarn showcases the intricate pattern stitch.

The stole assembly is simple, with the crochet patterns used as both an edging and an insertion (a piece made to join other pieces of fabric).

Sizing
Finished size: Approximately 42 x 18 in. (1m x 46cm) before fringing

Gauge
This project is worked to length and specific sizing is not necessary, so working to a gauge is not essential.

Materials
- **3** skeins* double-knit or light worsted yarn, main color (Microspun, Lion Brand Yarn Company, 168 yards per skein, Ebony #153)
- **2** skeins bulky yarn, accent color (Mystery, Lion Brand, 71 yards per ball, Fuchsia Facets#204)
- straight knitting needles, size 13 (9mm)
- crochet hook, size H-8 (5mm)
- tapestry or yarn needle
- tape measure
- yarn cutter
- * if not adding fringe, only 2 skeins of main-color yarn are needed

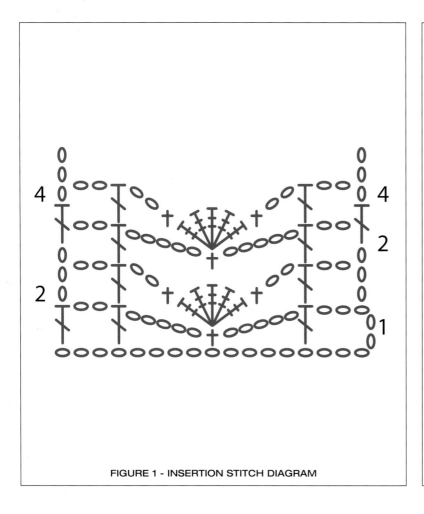

FIGURE 1 - INSERTION STITCH DIAGRAM

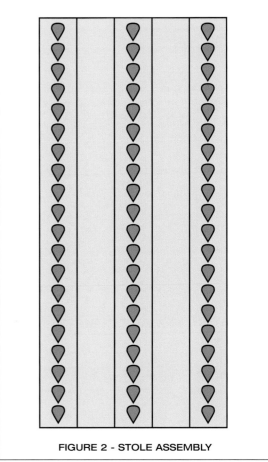

FIGURE 2 - STOLE ASSEMBLY

Make the knit strips

1 With knitting needles and accent yarn, CO 8 stitches. Work in garter stitch (k every row) until piece measures 42 in. (1m) and BO. Work in ends.

2 Repeat step 1 to make another strip.

Make the crochet strips

1 (See Figure 1.) With crochet hook and MC yarn, ch 21 loosely.
Row 1: Dc in 8th ch from hook, ch 5, skip next 4 chs, sc in next ch, ch 5, skip next 4 chs, dc in next ch, ch 2, skip next 2 chs, dc in last ch (4 ch-spaces).
Row 2 (right side): Ch 5 (counts as first dc plus ch 2, throughout), turn; dc in next dc, ch 2, sc in next ch 5 space, 5 tr in next sc, sc in next ch 5 space, ch 2, dc in next dc, ch 2, skip next 2 chs, dc in next ch.
Row 3: Ch 5, turn; dc in next dc, ch 5, skip next 2 tr, sc in next tr, ch 5, dc in next dc, ch 2, dc in beginning ch.

Row 4: Ch 5, turn; dc in next dc, ch 2, sc in next ch 5 space, 5 tr in next sc, sc in next ch 5 space, (ch 2, dc in next dc) twice.
2 Repeat rows 3 and 4 until piece measures the same length as knitted strips, end by working row 3, and fasten off. Work in ends.
3 Repeat steps 1–2 to make two more strips.

Assemble the stole

1 Using MC yarn and holding one crochet strip and one knit strip together, single crochet through both strips lengthwise to assemble. Alternate a crochet strip with a knit strip, using the photographs and Figure 2 as a guide.
2 To finish ends, attach MC yarn at corner, single crochet across each end, finish off, and work in ends.
3 Attach 5 in. (13cm) fringe, if desired.

Generally, insertions have the same edge on both sides and edgings are shaped along one side, but in this project, all three crochet panels match.

CREATIVE OPTIONS

Instead of a yarn fringe, attach tassels, ball fringe or upholstery trimmings to the ends.

Weave a ribbon through the center shells of the insertion panels.

Vary your yarn choices, both color and type, to completely change the look of the stole. Try a smooth worsted yarn for the knitted panels in the same tone as the crochet panels for an elegant look.

STITCH SPOTLIGHT

The garter stitch panels, done in a bright novelty yarn, are separated by a delicate crochet insertion.

Amazing autumn shawl

Colorful crocheted shapes embellish this textured shawl

Knit this shawl in alternating squares of stockinette and reverse stockinette that resemble a woven basket. (Think k 4, p 4 ribbing offset every four rows.) Visually appealing, there's also a practical advantage: The fabric remains flat and does not curl at the edges (as plain stockinette does), thus providing a good surface for embellishments.

Sizing
Finished size: Approximately 16 x 46 in. (41cm x 1.2m) before fringing

Gauge
Knit: 16 stitches/4 in. (10cm) over pattern stitch
Crochet: Leaves measure approximately 3¼ in. (8.3cm) long.

Materials
- **7** skeins worsted-weight yarn (Wool-Ease, Lion Brand Yarn Company, 197 yards per skein) in the following colors:
    3 skeins Autumn Print #233 (main color)
    skein Forest Green Heather #180
    skein Gold #171
    skein Cranberry #138
    skein Purple #147
- straight knitting needles, size 9 (5.5mm) or size to obtain gauge
- crochet hook, size G-6 (4mm)
- polyester batting, fiberfill, or cotton balls for stuffing berries
- tapestry or yarn needle
- tape measure
- yarn cutter

The basketweave texture is created by an alternating pattern of stockinette and reverse stockinette stitch.

Knit Pattern Stitch

(worked over a multiple of eight stitches)

Rows 1 through 4: *K4, p4, repeat from * across row.

Rows 5 through 8: *P4, k4, repeat from * across row. Repeat these eight rows for pattern.

Knit the shawl

1 With knitting needles and MC yarn, CO 72 stitches.

2 Work pattern stitch (one set of 8 rows) until piece measures approximately 46 in. (1.2m). End with row 8 of pattern and BO. Work in ends.

Crochet the embellishments

Using crochet hook and accent yarns, make embellishments as follows.

Berries (Make 36 total: 6 of Gold, 10 each of Forest Green Heather, Cranberry, and Purple)

1 Ch 6, join to form a ring.

Round 1: Ch 1 (counts as first sc), work 1 sc in first stitch, work 2 sc in each stitch around, join in beginning chain (12 stitches including beginning chain).

Rounds 2, 3 and 4: Ch 1 (beginning ch), skip first stitch, work 1 sc in each stitch around, join in beginning ch.

Round 5: Ch 1 (beginning chain), skip first stitch, work 2 sc together around, join in beginning chain. Fasten off, leaving an 8-in. (20cm) tail.

2 Stuff berry firmly with filling material.

Thread a tapestry needle with yarn tail and stitch around opening and draw closed. Knot yarn to secure, and use remaining yarn tail to attach berries to shawl in clusters of three.

Leaves (Make 48 total: 6 of Gold, 14 each of Forest Green Heather, Cranberry, and Purple)

1 Ch 16, work 1 sc in second chain from hook, 1 hdc in next ch, 1 dc in each of next 3 ch, 1 tr into each of next 4 ch, 1 dc into each of next 3 ch, 1 hdc into next ch and 1 sc into last ch.

2 Ch 3, then working into stitches on back of starting ch, work 1 sc in first ch, 1 hdc in next ch, 1 dc in each of next 3 ch, 1 tr into each of next 4 ch, 1 dc into each of next 3 ch, 1 hdc into next ch and 1 sc into last chain, join to beginning. Fasten off, leaving an 8-in. (20cm) tail to attach to shawl.

Tendrils (Make 32: 8 each of Forest Green Heather, Gold, Cranberry, and Purple)
Ch 30, work 1 hdc into third ch from hook, work 2 hdc into each ch to end. Fasten off, leaving an 8-in. (20cm) tail to attach to shawl.

Add the embellishments
Using the photograph as a placement guide, sew leaves to shawl in groups of two or three, then attach berries in clusters of three, and finally attach tendrils to clusters. Work in all ends, taking care to work embellishment yarn ends into like colors of leaves, berries, and tendrils.

CREATIVE OPTIONS

Make both the shawl and the embellishments in ecru or another neutral color for a classic, understated version.

Create a dramatic evening or holiday garment by selecting metallic yarn for the berries, leaves, and tendrils and white or black for the shawl.

Top the leaves and berries with beads.

The berries, tendrils, and leaves illustrate how simple crochet stitches – single, half-double, and double – can be used to produce sturdy, eye-catching, three-dimensional forms.

Retro loop boot toppers

Top a plain pair of boots with these stylish cuffs

Dress up a boot top without adding bulky socks. Knit these toppers in the round, using k 1, p 1 ribbing for a snug, flexible, and comfortable fit. The fun, textured crochet trim is worked in loop stitch, sometimes referred to as fur stitch.

These toppers are designed for over-the-calf boots. Vary the sizing by working a longer ribbing tube, or by casting on a few more stitches for a looser fit.

Sizing
Finished size: Approximately 6½ x 16 in. (17 x 41cm) circumference at top

Gauge
Knit: 26 stitches/4 in. (10cm) in k 1, p 1 ribbing

Materials
- skein worsted-weight yarn, main color (Wool-Ease, Lion Brand Yarn Company, 197 yards per skein, Mink Brown #127)
- skein bulky-weight yarn, accent color (Lion Suede, Lion Brand, 122 yards per skein, Ecru #210)
- double-pointed knitting needles, size 6 (4mm) or size to obtain gauge
- crochet hook, size J-10 (6mm)
- tapestry or yarn needle
- tape measure
- yarn cutter

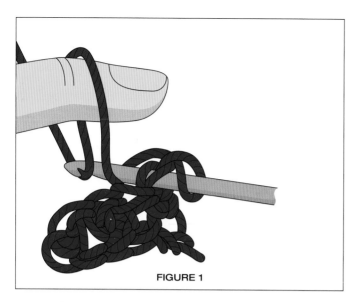

FIGURE 1

Crochet Technique Note

Loop stitch: This stitch is a variation of single crochet and is usually worked on wrong-side rows as the loops form to the back of the work. The yarn can be cut later and the resulting fabric will resemble fur. Use caution and test first, as some yarns will ravel when cut.

Step 1: Using left index finger to control loop size, insert the hook, pick up both threads of the loop and draw through (see Figure 1).

Step 2: Wrap the ball yarn around hook.

Step 3: Draw yarn through all loops on hook to complete and lock loop in place (see Figures 2 and 3).

Knit the cuff body

1 With double-pointed needles and MC yarn, CO 74 stitches.

2 Join to work in the round and work k 1, p 1 ribbing until piece measures 5 in. (13cm). BO in rib.

3 Repeat steps 1–2 to make a second cuff body.

Crochet the cuff top

1 Using crochet hook and accent color yarn, attach to top edge.

Round 1: Ch 1, * sc in every other knit stitch around, join to beginning ch, ch 1, turn.

Round 2: Work loop stitch in every sc around, join, **do not** turn.

Rounds 3 and 4: Work as for round 2 and fasten off. Work in all ends.

2 Repeat on the second cuff.

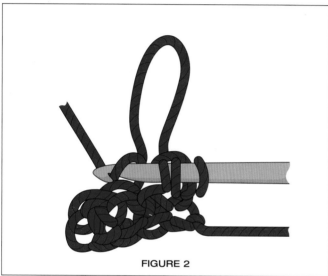

FIGURE 2

Two or three ply? "Ply" refers to the number of threads that are twisted together to make up a strand of yarn. The number of plies doesn't affect the weight of the yarn, but it can affect how much loft the yarn has.

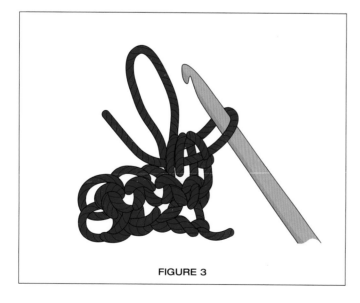

FIGURE 3

The cuff is made in knit 1 purl 1 ribbing for a close fit; the crocheted loop stitch trim adds drama.

CREATIVE OPTIONS

Work rounds of single crochet at the top instead of loop stitch and then attach embellishments such as buttons or pom poms to the top.

Vary the colors to coordinate with your wardrobe. For a different look, use a fur yarn for the loop trim. Depending on the color, the look can be very natural or completely fun.

Easy tubey socks

Keep your tootsies toasty with these easy-to-make socks

These eye-catching socks are simple knitted tubes with some shaping at the toe. This allows a comfortable, flattering fit without the difficulty of turning a heel. Now, making socks doesn't sound so scary, after all. You might even be inspired to make some for family and friends; both the foot and cuff can be made any length desired to customize the fit.

Use a fun and fancy novelty yarn to create a cuff in easy half-double crochet.

Sizing
Finished size: Women's shoe size 7 to 9

Gauge
26 stitches/4 in. (10cm) in k 1, p 1 ribbing

Materials
- skein worsted-weight yarn, main color (Wool-Ease, Lion Brand Yarn Company, 197 yards per skein, Fuchsia #137)
- skein eyelash yarn, accent color (Fancy Fur, Lion Brand, 39 yards per skein, Spring Garden #294)
- double-pointed knitting needles, size 6 (4mm) or size needed to obtain gauge
- crochet hook, size J-10 (6mm)
- tapestry or yarn needle
- tape measure
- yarn cutter

Choose your colors with abandon or keep them subdued for very different looks.

Try different novelty yarns, such as suede, for the cuff. Be sure to test first, as you may need to vary the number of stitches picked up.

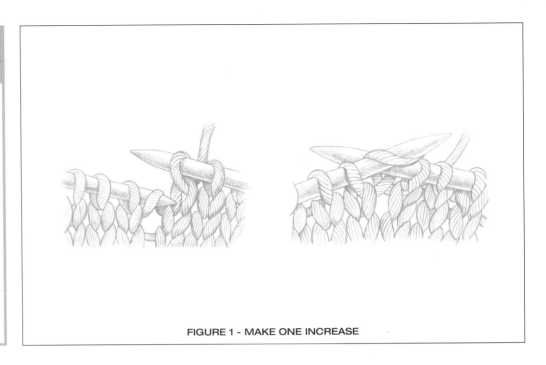

FIGURE 1 - MAKE ONE INCREASE

Adjust the size of these socks by using a smaller or larger needle, or by knitting a longer or shorter tube.

Technique Notes

• *When increasing two stitches at once, work one in knit and one in purl to correspond to the ribbing pattern.*

• *To prevent a hole in the knitting, make the first increase by pulling up a new stitch from the stitch below the row you are on (see Figure 1). Make the second increase by working into the front and back of the same stitch (a bar increase, see Basics).*

Knit the sock

(worked from toe to cuff)

1 With double-pointed needles and MC yarn, CO on 30 stitches. Join to work in the round, mark beginning of round, and work k 1, p 1 ribbing until piece measures 2 in. (5cm).

2 Increase for foot: Continue in ribbing, and at beginning of round *work 2 stitches in rib, inc 2 stitches, work 4 stitches in rib, inc 2 stitches, repeat from * around ending with 2 stitches in rib pattern (50 stitches).

3 Work even in ribbing until piece measures 12 in. (30cm) or desired length. BO loosely in rib.

4 Repeat steps 1–3 to make a second sock.

Crochet the cuff

1 Using crochet hook and accent color yarn, attach yarn to top edge of sock.

Round 1: Ch 1, * sc in every other knit stitch around, join to beginning ch.

Round 2: Ch 2 (counts as first hdc), work hdc in each stitch around, join at top of beginning ch 2.

Rounds 3 through 6: Work as for round 2 and fasten off.

2 Repeat to add a cuff to the second sock.

Finish the sock

Sew toe closed and work in all ends. Finish the second sock in the same way.

Use novelty yarn for the single-crochet cuff; knit 1 purl 1 ribbing creates a snug-fitting sock.

Terrific tote

Pack your needlework and the rest of your essentials into this roomy tote

Thick yarns and large tools mean this bag works up quickly. Knit the body in stockinette stitch, adding shaping at the sides for a roomier interior. A single crochet band at the top stiffens the opening, so the bag is easy to open and close. The frame and handles, also crocheted, are sturdy and practical. The novelty yarn is fun and decorative, but the frame provides structural support, and single crochet gives the necessary added strength: It's a perfect choice to hold your thick yarn and large tools!

Sizing
Finished size: approximately 21 in. (53cm) long and 10 in. (25cm) deep

Gauge
Knit: 9 stitches/4 in. (10cm) in stockinette stitch
Crochet: 7 sc/4 in. (10cm)

Materials
- **2** skeins super-bulky yarn, main color (Wool-Ease Thick & Quick, Lion Brand Yarn Company, 108 yards per skein, Plum #145)
- **4** skeins super-bulky yarn, accent color (Fettuccini, Lion Brand, 33 yards per ball, Eden #201)
- **4** silver cinchers (JHB International, Inc., #09353)
- straight knitting needles, size 13 (9mm) or size needed to obtain gauge
- crochet hook, size N (10mm) or size needed to obtain gauge
- tapestry or yarn needle
- tape measure
- yarn cutter

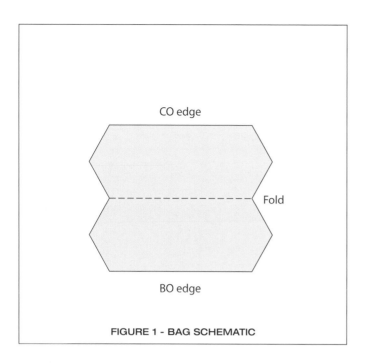

CO edge

Fold

BO edge

FIGURE 1 - BAG SCHEMATIC

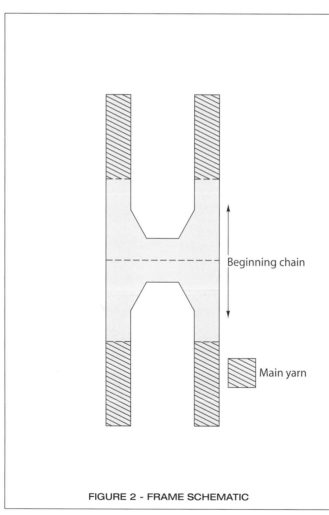

Beginning chain

Main yarn

FIGURE 2 - FRAME SCHEMATIC

Knit the bag body

1 With knitting needles and MC yarn, CO 34 stitches.
K 1 row, p 1 row.
2 Begin increases all on right-side rows: Keeping first stitch in stockinette (work increases one stitch in from edge), inc 1 stitch each end to 48 stitches.
3 Work one purl row.
4 Begin decreases all on right-side rows: Again, keeping first stitch in stockinette (work decreases one stitch in from edge), dec 1 stitch each end to 34 stitches.
5 Work one purl row.
6 Repeat steps 2–5 once. BO all stitches. (See Figure 1.)
7 Fold bag in half width-wise and sew side seams (CO and BO edges are together). When sewing seam, be sure to take up only one half of edge stitches. Otherwise, the bag will be too small and the seam too bulky.

Crochet the top edge

1 With MC yarn and crochet hook, attach yarn to top of bag at side seam. Ch 1, work one sc in each stitch around, join to ch 1 with slip stitch (66 stitches, including ch 1).
2 Work three rounds more of sc for a total of four sc rounds. Fasten off and work in ends.

Crochet the frame

1 With accent color yarn and crochet hook, ch 36, skip 1 ch, sc in each ch to end, turn, ch 1 (35 sc).
2 Work four rows even.
3 Begin handle shaping: On next row, work 10 sc across, turn.
Decrease row: Ch 1, 2 sc together, sc to end, turn.
Plain row: Ch 1, sc across (10 sc including turning ch).
Repeat decease row and plain row until 5 sc (including turning chain) remain.
4 Work even on 5 stitches until handle measures 13 in. (33cm) from beginning.

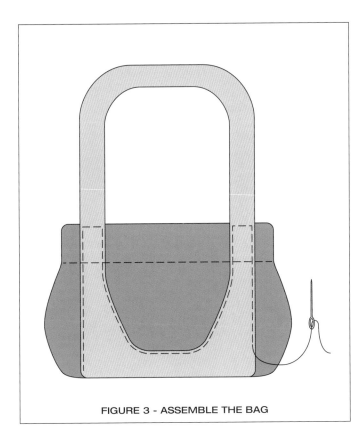

FIGURE 3 - ASSEMBLE THE BAG

5 Attach main yarn, continue even in sc until handle measures 22 in. (56cm) from beginning or desired length.
6 At outside edge, attach accent color yarn and sc across 10 stitches at top edge.
7 Begin at decrease rows in step 3 above, and repeat through step 5.
8 To create the frame on the back of the bag, attach accent color yarn to opposite side of starting ch 36, ch 1, sc in each ch to end, turn, ch 1 (35 sc).
9 Work four rows even.
10 Repeat handle shaping (steps 3–7) to complete remaining straps. Work in all ends (see Figure 2).

Assemble and finish the bag
1 Sew short ends of same-side handles together to join.
2 Insert bag into frame and sew along frame edges to secure (see Figure 3). (Put a magazine inside the bag to help avoid sewing through both layers.)
3 Attach cincher rings to either side of frame on front of bag.
4 With accent yarn, lace the rings, tie, and attach 5½ in. (14cm) tassel to handle.

When working with hand-dyed or self-striping yarns, watch the color and pattern when joining new yarns. Take care to join in the same color sequence as the old for a less jarring change.

CREATIVE OPTIONS

Instead of lacings, use buttons and tabs: Ch 6, sc in second ch from hook and each ch across, ch 1, turn. Work even on 5 sc until tab measures 4 in. (10cm). Sc2tog, sc2tog, ch 1, turn (3 sc). Sc2tog (2 sc), turn and work last two stitches together. Fasten off and work in ends. Sew tab to side of bag. Sew button on top of shaped end of tab.

Work the body of the bag in a striped pattern. Every two rows (on each right side row), change colors. Alternate two colors or stitch a whole rainbow to coordinate with your accent yarn.

Attach tassels to all four handles at the top of the bag. Add sparkle by embellishing the tassels with beads.

Sassy summer vest

Wear this light and cool vest over a tank top or as a beach cover-up

This pullover tank-style vest features a knitted yoke and a crocheted bottom and edging. Subtly shaped stockinette stitch gives the yoke a smooth texture. The vest bodice showcases an eye-catching openwork stitch, with picots to highlight the edging. Worked in the round, the pattern stitch forms a gentle and very flattering diagonal fan pattern.

Sizing
Finished size: 36 (40, 44) in./ .9 (1, 1.1m) at chest; larger sizes in parentheses

Gauge
Knit: 15 stitches/4 in. (10cm) in stockinette stitch
Crochet: 5 double crochet stitches/1 in. (2.5cm)

Materials
- **3** skeins worsted-weight yarn (Lion Cotton, Lion Brand Yarn Company, 236 yards per skein, Periwinkle #183)
- clasp (Ingrid Clasp, Pewter, JHB International, Inc., #00976)
- 54 in. (1.4m) ½-in. (1.3cm) wide ribbon
- straight knitting needles, size 8 (5mm) or size needed to obtain gauge
- crochet hook, size G-6 (4mm) or size needed to obtain gauge
- tapestry or yarn needle
- tape measure
- scissors
- sewing thread and needle

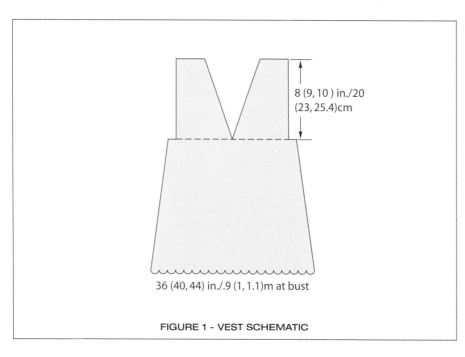

FIGURE 1 - VEST SCHEMATIC

8 (9, 10) in./20 (23, 25.4)cm

36 (40, 44) in./.9 (1, 1.1)m at bust

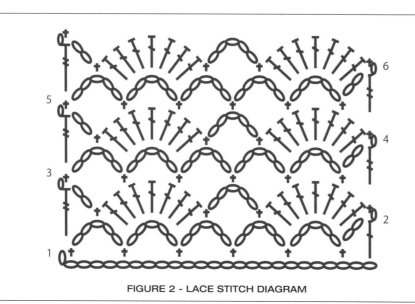

FIGURE 2 - LACE STITCH DIAGRAM

CREATIVE OPTIONS

Work the top and bottom in different colors. Try a soft combination of white and a pastel, or go with black and a bright. Work the yoke in color A, and work the crochet rounds in alternating color A and B.

Work pattern rounds of the vest bodice in multiple colors for a wave-like effect.

Sew beads randomly across the yoke and at the picot points on the edging.

Crochet Pattern Stitch

Fan and Trellis stitch, a multiple of 12 stitches plus 11. When working flat, add 1 for base chain.

Foundation chain: Ch a multiple of 12, plus 11 ch.

Row 1 (wrong side): 1 sc into 2nd ch from hook, *ch 5, skip 3 ch, 1 sc into next ch; repeat from * to last 2 ch, ch 2, skip 1 ch, 1 dc into last ch, turn.

Row 2: Ch 1, 1 sc into first stitch, skip 2 ch sp,* 7 dc into next 5ch arch, 1 sc into next arch †, ch 5, 1 sc into next arch; repeat from * ending last repeat at †, 2 ch, 1 tr into last sc, skip turning ch, turn.

Row 3: Ch 1, 1 sc into first stitch, *ch 5, 1 sc into 2nd of next 7 dc, ch 5, 1 sc into 6th dc of same group †, ch 5, 1 sc into next 5 ch arch; repeat from * ending last repeat at † , ch 2, 1 tr into last sc, skip turning ch, turn.

Repeat rows 2 and 3 for pattern. (See Figure 2.)

Knit the yoke back

1 With knitting needles, CO 56 (64, 68) stitches.

2 Work in stockinette stitch until piece measures 8 (9, 10) in./20 (23, 25) cm.

3 Begin neck shaping (work both sides at once by attaching a second ball of yarn after center stitches are bound off): Work across 23 (27, 28) stitches. BO center 10 (10, 12) stitches.

4 Attach second ball of yarn and work to end of row.

5 Continue neck shaping by BO at both sides of neck edge two stitches next five rows. BO remaining shoulder stitches.

Knit the yoke fronts

1 With knitting needles, CO 28 (32, 34) stitches.

2 Work in stockinette stitch for four rows.

3 Begin front neck shaping (keep one stitch at neck edge in stockinette stitch by making decrease one stitch in from edge): At neck edge decrease one stitch every third row to 13 (17, 18) stitches.

4 Work even until armhole edge measures 9 (10, 11) in./23 (25, 28) cm. BO remaining shoulder stitches.

5 Make second front but reverse shaping by working neck edge on other side.

Crochet the vest bottom

1 Starting at bottom edge of back, with right side facing, attach yarn. Work 1 sc in each knit stitch across.

2 At end of piece, ch 10 (14, 16) attach right front and sc across bottom edge.

3 At end of piece, attach left front and continue across with 1 sc in each knit stitch.

4 At end of left front, ch 10 (14, 16) and attach to beginning edge of back with a slip stitch. Total stitches: 132 (156, 168). Check the alignment of the front and back bodice pieces. They should be untwisted, with right sides out and attached at the bottom with the stitches just worked.

5 Begin pattern stitch, worked in rounds, with a multiple of 12 stitches. You will work with the right side facing – do not turn the work.

The pattern worked in rounds will form a gentle and flattering diagonal or spiral around the vest bottom.

Round 1: 1 sc into 1st sc, *ch 5, skip 3 sc, 1 sc into next sc; repeat from * to last 3 sc, ch 2, skip 3 sc, 1 dc into first sc.

Round 2: Ch 1, 1 sc into previous stitch, * 7 dc into next 5ch arch, 1 sc into next arch †, ch 5, 1 sc into next 5 ch arch, repeat from * ending last repeat at †, ch 2, 1 tr into first sc.

Round 3: Ch 1, 1 sc into previous stitch, * ch 5, 1 sc into 2nd of next 7 dc, ch 5, 1 sc into 6th of same dc group †, ch 5, 1 sc into next ch 5 arch, repeat from * ending last repeat at †, ch 2, 1 tr into first sc.

6 Repeat pattern rounds 2 and 3 three times, then round 2 once.

7 Work increase rounds:

Round 11: Ch 1, 1 sc into previous stitch, * ch 7, 1 sc into 2nd of next 7 dc, ch 7, 1 sc into 6th of same dc group †, ch 7, 1 sc into next ch 5 arch, repeat from * ending last repeat at †, ch 3, 1 tr into first sc.

Round 12: Ch 1, 1 sc into previous stitch, skip ch 3 sp,* 9 dc into next 7 ch arch, 1 sc into next arch †, ch 7, 1 sc into next 7 ch arch, repeat from * ending last repeat at †, ch 3, 1 tr into first sc.

Round 13: Ch 1, 1 sc into previous stitch, * ch 7, 1 sc into 2nd of next 9 dc, ch 7, 1 sc into 8th of same dc group †, ch 7, 1 sc into next ch 7 arch, repeat from * ending last repeat at †, ch 3, 1 tr into first sc.

8 Repeat rounds 12 and 13 another eight times or until crochet portion measures approximately 15 in. (38cm) or desired length. End with round 13. (See Figure 1.)

Crochet the edging

Ch 1, * work 7 sc in next ch 7 arch, 1 sc in next sc, 1 sc in next 5 dc, ch 3, sc in same sc (picot made), 1 sc in next 4 dc, 1 sc in next sc, repeat from * around. End with slip stitch in beginning ch 1. Fasten off. Work in all ends.

Finish the vest

1 Work sc around armhole and neck openings.

2 Thread ribbon tie though bottom of bodice, tie, and trim to desired length.

3 Attach clasp at bottom of neck opening.

Cotton fibers come from the seed pod, or boll, of the cotton plant, which is grown in hot climates worldwide. It is absorbent and doesn't attract moths, but 100% cotton yarns can be heavy and lack resilience.

STITCH SPOTLIGHT

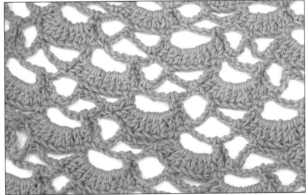

The yoke is knit in smooth stockinette stitch; the crocheted portion is a diagonal fan pattern.

Winter vest

A "cruelty-free" collar tops a flattering, form-fitting vest

Work the body of this vest entirely in k 2, p 2 ribbing, using smaller needles to knit the waist portion for a sleek, body-conscious fit. The edge-to-edge front closure simplifies the finishing, and the pattern stitch creates a clean, self-finished lower edge.

The real focus is the attention-getting collar. The pattern stitch, Astrakhan stitch, has been a wonderful substitute for real fur pelts for years. (Additionally, it's a great example of a crochet stitch achieving a look than may not be possible, or at least as easily worked, in knitting.)

Sizing
Finished size: 37 (39, 41) in./.94 (.99, 1) m at chest; larger sizes in parentheses

Gauge
Knit: 20 stitches/4 in. (10.2cm) in k 2, p 2 ribbing, slightly stretched on larger needles
Crochet: 8 stitches/2 in. (5cm) over pattern stitch

Materials
- **3 (4, 4)** skeins worsted-weight yarn, main color (Wool-Ease, Lion Brand Yarn Company, 185 yards per skein: Oxford Grey #152)
- **2** skeins worsted-weight yarn, accent color (Wool-Ease, Lion Brand, Wheat #402)
- straight knitting needles, sizes 6 (4mm) and 8 (5mm) or sizes needed to obtain gauge
- crochet hook, size G-6 (4mm) or size needed to obtain gauge
- **3** silver clasps (Alpine Clasp, Antique Silver, JHB International Inc., #00892)
- tapestry or yarn needle
- tape measure
- scissors
- sewing thread and needle

Because this garment is so fitted, be sure to select a size with adequate ease – this vest is meant to be form fitting but not skintight. I recommend ½-2 in. (2.5-5cm) of ease.

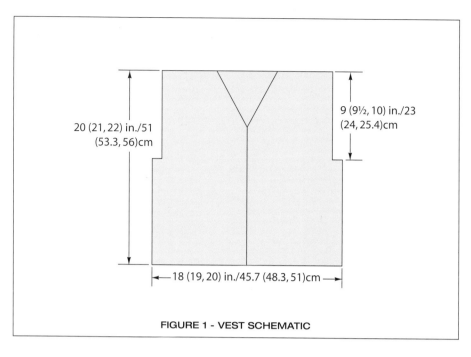

20 (21, 22) in./51 (53.3, 56)cm

9 (9½, 10) in./23 (24, 25.4)cm

18 (19, 20) in./45.7 (48.3, 51)cm

FIGURE 1 - VEST SCHEMATIC

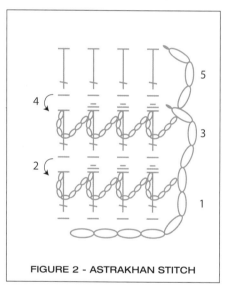

FIGURE 2 - ASTRAKHAN STITCH

Crochet Pattern Stitch

Astrakhan stitch, worked over a multiple of any number of stitches.

Technique Note:

*This method of working is a variation of traditional Astrakhan stitch, which allows you to turn the work and work each row in the usual direction. Rows 2 and 3 will be worked in the front and back loops of the **same** row below. You will have worked across that row twice.*

Foundation chain: Ch desired number of stitches, plus 3 ch.
*Row 1: Skip 3 ch (counts as 1 dc), * 1 dc into each ch to end, turn.*
*Row 2: *Ch 7, slip stitch into back loop (farthest from you) of next dc, repeat from * across, ending ch 7 slip stitch into third ch of turning ch, turn.*
Row 3: Ch 3 (counts as 1 dc), skip 1 dc, dc into back loop of next dc (the ch 7 loop is in the front loop of the dc, you are working into the row twice). Work 1 dc in each stitch across, turn.
Repeat rows 2 and 3 for pattern (see Figure 2).

Knit the vest back

1 With larger needles and MC color, CO 92 (96, 104) stitches.
2 Work in k 2, p 2 ribbing until piece measures 5 (5½, 6) in./13 (14, 15) cm.

3 Switch to smaller needles and work until piece measures 11 (11.5, 12) in./28 (29.2, 30) cm.
4 Work underarm decrease: BO 4 stitches at each edge (84, 88, 96 stitches).
5 Switch back to larger needles and work even to 20 (21, 22) in./51 (53, 56) cm. BO in rib stitch and work in ends.

Knit the vest fronts

1 With larger needles and MC, CO 46 (48, 52) stitches.
2 Work in k 2, p 2 ribbing until piece measures 5 (5½, 6) in./13 (14, 15) cm.
3 Switch to smaller needles and work until piece measures 11 (11½, 12) in./28 (29.2, 30) cm.
4 Work underarm decrease: BO 4 stitches at arm edge (42, 44, 48 stitches).
5 Switch back to larger needles, work even in ribbing to 14 (14½, 15) in./36 (36.8, 38) cm and begin neck shaping.
6 At neck edge, BO 2 stitches every other row five (six, seven) times, then decrease 1 stitch once (once, no decrease) (31, 32, 34 stitches).
7 Work even in ribbing to 21 (21, 22) in./51 (53, 56) cm. BO in rib and work in ends. Repeat steps 1–7 to make a second piece, and sew shoulder seams (see Figure 1).

Crochet the collar

1 With crochet hook and accent color and right side of work facing you, attach yarn to neck edge. Ch 1 and work 1 sc into each knit stitch and row around neck edge, ch 3, turn. Note: Collar will fold over vest, so wrong side of collar is against right side of vest.

Row 1: 1 dc in each sc, turn.

Row 2 (6, 10 and 14) (right-side row): *Ch 7, slip stitch into back loop (farthest from you) of next dc, repeat from * across, ending ch 7 slip stitch into third ch of turning ch, turn.

Row 3 (7 and 11): Ch 3 (counts as 1 dc), skip 1 dc, dc into back loop of next dc (the ch 7 loop is in the front loop of the dc, you are working into the row twice). Work 1 dc in each stitch across, turn.

Row 4 (8 and 12): Repeat row 2.

Row 5 (9 and 13) (increase rows): Ch 3, skip 1 dc, dc into back loop of next 2 dc, 2 dc into back loop of next dc, repeat across, turn.

2 Repeat rows 2, 3, 4 and 5 to row 13. For row 14, repeat row 2 once, fasten off, and work in ends.

Finish the vest

1 Sew side seams.

2 With crochet hook and MC yarn, pick up stitches around arm edges, join, work one round sc.

3 Attach MC yarn to front edge and work one row sc. Repeat for other side.

4 Attach closures to front edges.

Knit 2, purl 2 ribbing creates a stretchy, form-fitting fabric; Astrakhan stitch, often used to imitate the texture of fur, is a prime example of crochet's versatility.

STITCH SPOTLIGHT

CREATIVE OPTIONS

Go for a playful palette instead of natural look. Try a black body with a bright collar (fuchsia, for example), then finish off with large matching buttons fastened with chain loops.

Use a white fuzzy yarn for the collar, then scatter black buttons on it for a faux ermine look.

Sultry skirt

Wear this lacy feminine piece as an overskirt – or not, if you dare!

This skirt, a stylish addition to your year-round wardrobe, is knit in the round from the waist down. Work the yoke in k 1, p 1 ribbing for a smooth fit. The bottom portion is crocheted in the round down to the finished edge. Achieve increases in circumference by increasing needle and hook sizes.

For a flattering fit, this skirt should measure 2–4 in. (5–10cm) more than your hip measurement, with more ease in the larger sizes. Choose your finished size accordingly. The skirt sits about 1 in. (2.5cm) below your natural waist. If you wish to adjust the yoke length for modesty, work in the k 1, p 1 ribbing as desired, and then adjust the finished length as well.

Sizing
Finished size: 38 (42, 46) in./.97 (1, 1.2) m at hip

Gauge
Knit: 18 stitches/4 in. (10cm) on larger needles
Crochet: 2 pattern repeats/3½ in. (8.9cm) in pattern stitch

Materials
- **4 (5, 5)** skeins worsted-weight yarn (Wool-Ease, Lion Brand Yarn Company, 197 yards per skein, Black # 153)
- circular knitting needles, sizes 6 (4mm) and 8 (5mm) or size needed to obtain gauge over k 1, p 1 ribbing
- crochet hooks, sizes G-6 (4mm) and I-9 (5.5mm) or sizes needed to obtain gauge over pattern stitch
- ribbon or cording for waist tie
- tapestry or yarn needle
- tape measure
- yarn cutter

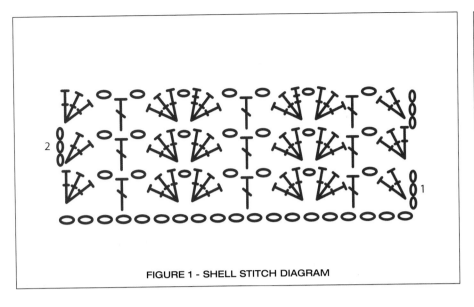

FIGURE 1 - SHELL STITCH DIAGRAM

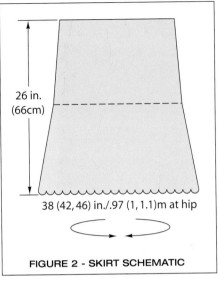

26 in. (66cm)

38 (42, 46) in./.97 (1, 1.1)m at hip

FIGURE 2 - SKIRT SCHEMATIC

Stretch factor —
Hand-knitted fabric has a tendency to stretch lengthwise more than crosswise. That means a sweater or skirt may get longer as you wear it. With some yarns, such as cotton or linen, the change can be dramatic over the course of a day.

Pattern Stitch

The pattern stitch is worked over a multiple of 7 stitches plus 4.

Row 1: Ch 3, 2 dc in 4th ch from hook, ch 1, skip 2 ch, 1 dc in next ch, ch 1, *skip 2 ch, (3 dc, ch 1, 3 dc) in next ch (shell made), ch 1, skip 2 ch, 1 dc in next ch, ch 1, repeat from * across and end 3 dc in last ch, ch 3, turn.

Row 2: 2 dc in 1st dc, ch 1, skip (2 dc, ch 1), * 1 dc in next dc, ch1, skip (ch 1, 3 dc), 1 shell in next ch 1 space (center of previous shell), ch 1, skip (3 dc, ch1), repeat from * across and end 3 dc in turning chain of previous row, ch 3, turn.

Repeat row 2 for pattern (see Figure 1).

Knit the yoke

1 With smaller needles, CO 172 (190, 220) stitches. Join to work in round. (Be sure that stitches are not twisted – check again at the end of the first round. You can still save it at this point; work any further and you must rip if it is twisted.)

2 Work in k 1, p 1 ribbing for 7 (8, 10) in./18 (20, 25) cm.

3 Switch to larger needles and continue in ribbing until yoke measures 13 (14, 15) in./33 (35.5, 38) cm or desired length. BO loosely in pattern. Work in ends.

Use different colors of yarn for each crochet round on the bottom for sassy stripes.

Add fringe to the bottom of the skirt.

This skirt can be a summer or winter basic depending on the yarn you use. Try a worsted-weight cotton yarn for summer. Be sure to check your gauge!

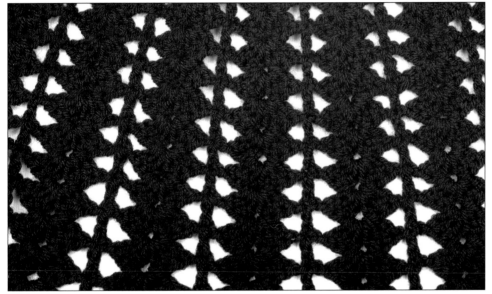

Knit 1, purl 1 ribbing creates a smooth, fitted yoke; the crocheted shell lace makes a flouncy skirt.

Crochet the skirt bottom

1 With smaller crochet hook and right side of skirt facing you, attach yarn to bound off (bottom) edge, ch 1, sc in each stitch around (172, 190, 220), join to beginning ch 1. Begin pattern rounds. (On first pattern round, adjust stitches if necessary to accommodate pattern by skipping more or fewer picked up stitches.)

Round 1: Ch 3, 2 dc in 1st sc, ch 1, skip 2 sc, 1 dc in next sc, ch 1, *skip 2 sc, (3 dc, ch 1, 3 dc) in next sc (shell made), ch 1, skip 2 sc, 1 dc in next sc, ch 1, repeat from * around and end 3 dc in 1st sc, ch 1, join to top of beginning ch 3. DO NOT TURN. You will work every round from the right side.

Round 2: Ch 3, 2 dc in 1st dc, ch 1, skip (2 dc, ch 1), * 1 dc in next dc, ch 1, skip (ch 1, 3 dc), 1 shell in next ch 1 space (center of previous shell), ch 1, skip (3dc, ch 1), repeat from * around and end 3 dc in ch 1 space of previous round, ch 1, join to top of beginning ch 3.

2 Work Round 2 of pattern 14 more times for 15 pattern rounds.

3 Switch to larger crochet hook and work 12 more rounds (total 27 rounds) or until desired length. End off and work in ends (see Figure 2).

Finish the skirt

Thread ribbon or cord through ribbing at waist.

Tropical summer shrug

Top off a summer outfit with this soft, pretty, and feminine shrug

Make a stunning shrug with a short bodice, shiny buttons, and dramatic sleeves. Seed stitch, a non-curling pattern stitch, gives the bodice a soft fit, flattering drape, and subtle texture. The sleeve caps are crocheted in a lace pattern, gently shaped with short rows inside the edges. Add a simple single crochet edging, with picot loops around the neck, fronts, and bottom.

Sizing
Finished size: 40 (44, 48) in./ 1 (1.1, 1.2) m at chest; larger sizes in parentheses

Gauge
Knit: 18 stitches/4 in. (10cm) in seed stitch
Crochet: 2 pattern repeats/ 2¾ in. (7cm) in pattern stitch

Materials
- **4 (5, 5)** skeins light worsted or double-knit yarn (Microspun, Lion Brand Yarn Company, 168 yards per skein, Mango #186)
- straight knitting needles, size 6 (4mm) or size needed to obtain gauge
- crochet hook, size F (3.75mm) or size to obtain gauge
- **3** buttons (Sunfire Buttons, Gold, JHB International, Inc., #90025)
- tapestry or yarn needle
- tape measure
- yarn cutter
- sewing thread and needle

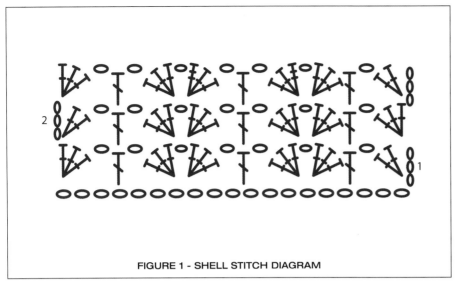

FIGURE 1 - SHELL STITCH DIAGRAM

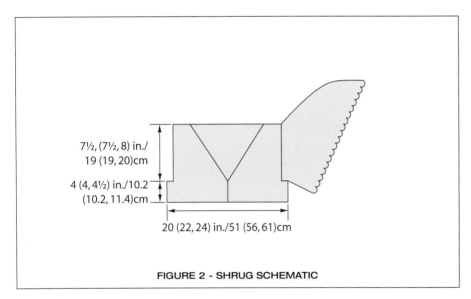

7½, (7½, 8) in./
19 (19, 20)cm

4 (4, 4½) in./10.2
(10.2, 11.4)cm

20 (22, 24) in./51 (56, 61)cm

FIGURE 2 - SHRUG SCHEMATIC

Knit Pattern Stitch

Seed stitch:
Cast on desired number of stitches.
Work k 1, p 1 across row.
On the next row, work the opposite of the stitch in the row below.
Repeat for pattern.

Crochet Pattern Stitch

The pattern stitch is worked over a multiple of 7 stitches plus 4.
Row 1: Ch 3, 2 dc in 4th ch from hook, ch 1, skip 2 ch, 1 dc in next ch, ch 1, *skip 2 ch, (3 dc, ch 1, 3 dc) in next ch (shell made), ch 1, skip 2 ch, 1 dc in next ch, ch 1, repeat from * across and end 3 dc in last ch, ch 3, turn.
Row 2: 2 dc in 1st dc, ch 1, skip (2 dc, ch 1), * 1 dc in next dc, ch1, skip (ch 1, 3 dc), 1 shell in next ch 1 space (center of

previous shell), ch 1, skip (3 dc, ch 1), repeat from * across and end 3 dc in turning chain of previous row, ch 3, turn. Repeat row 2 for pattern (see Figure 1).

Knit the shrug back

1 With knitting needles, CO 72 (81, 86) stitches.
2 Work in seed stitch until piece measures 4 (4, 4½) in./10 (10, 11.4) cm.
3 Shape armholes: BO 5 stitches on each side (62, 71, 76 stitches).
4 Work even in pattern to 11½ (11½, 12½) in./29 (29, 31.7) cm.
5 Begin neck shaping (work both sides at once by attaching a second ball of yarn after center stitches are bound off): Work across 13 (17, 19) stitches. BO center 36 (37, 38) stitches. Attach second ball of yarn and work to end of row.

6 Work even in pattern to 12 (12, 13) in./30 (30, 33) cm. BO remaining 13 (19, 19) shoulder stitches each side.

Knit the shrug fronts

1 With knitting needles, CO 36 (41, 43) stitches.
2 Work in seed stitch until piece measures 4 (4, 4½) in./10 (10, 11.4) cm.
3 Shape armhole: BO 5 stitches at arm edge (31, 36, 38 stitches).
4 Begin front neck shaping: At neck edge decrease one stitch every third row to 13 (17, 19) stitches.
5 Work even until armhole edge measures 8 (8, 8½) in./20 (20, 21.6) cm. BO remaining 13 (17, 19) shoulder stitches.
6 Make a second front to match the first. This stitch is reversible so there is no need to reverse shaping; just turn one over to make left and right fronts.
7 Sew shoulder and side seams (see Figure 2).

Crochet the sleeves

1 Starting at bottom side of armhole opening, with right side facing, attach yarn with crochet hook. Work 1 sc in each stitch around armhole (133, 133, 140 stitches). Do not work across bottom of opening.

On first pattern row, adjust stitches if necessary to accommodate pattern by skipping more or fewer picked up stitches.
Row 1: Ch 3, turn, 2 dc in 1st sc, ch 1, skip 2 sc, 1 dc in next sc, ch 1, *skip 2 sc, (3 dc, ch 1, 3 dc) in next sc (shell made), ch 1, skip 2 sc, 1 dc in next sc, ch 1, repeat from * across and end 3 dc in last sc, ch 3, turn.
Row 2: 2 dc in 1st dc, ch 1, skip (2 dc, ch 1), * 1 dc in next dc, ch1, skip (ch 1, 3dc), 1 shell in next ch 1 space (center of previous shell), ch 1, skip (3 dc, ch 1), repeat from * across and end 3 dc in turning chain of previous row, ch 3, turn.
Row 3: 2 dc in 1st dc, ch 1, skip (2 dc, ch 1), * 1 dc in next dc, ch 1, skip (ch 1, 3 dc), 1 shell in next ch 1 space (center of previous shell), ch 1, skip (3 dc, ch 1), repeat from * 1 more time, ** 1 dc in next dc, ch 1, skip (ch 1, 3 dc), (3 trc, ch 2, 3 trc) in next sp (long shell made in center of previous shell), ch 1, skip (3 dc, ch 1), repeat from ** 14 (14, 15) more times, repeat instructions between

Work sleeves and edging in a contrasting color. Try a soft combination of white and a pastel, or go with black and a bright.

Thread narrow ribbon vertically through the centers of the shells in the sleeves.

Attach beads, buttons, or ribbon roses to picot loops on bottom.

Sew beads randomly across the bodice and at the picot points on the edging.

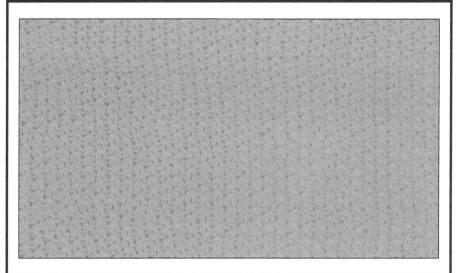

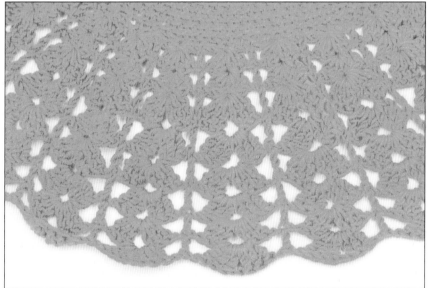

The bodice fabric is made from knitted seed stitch and the sleeves are crocheted shell lace.

"Squishy" balls — Wind your yarn loosely to make sure it doesn't stretch during winding – if it does, it will shrink back when washed. Wrap the yarn around your fingers as you wind and pull your fingers out when you reposition the ball. This allows the yarn to relax in the ball.

* two more times and end 3 dc in turning chain of previous row, ch 3, turn.
2 Repeat row 3 five more times. Fasten off and work in all ends.

Add crochet edging
With right side facing, attach yarn and work 5 sc, 3 ch around bottom, fronts and neck edge. Join with slip stitch.

Finish the shrug
Buttons are evenly spaced along front edge with one at top and bottom.
1 Using the crochet hook and on the wrong side, attach yarn to right front at top edge of front opening. * Ch 10 for first button loop, slip stitch to front in next sc. Slip stitch along wrong side of front to next button location. Repeat from * to last button loop and end with slip stitch to front. Fasten off and work ends in.
2 Attach buttons to left front on sc band to correspond to ch 10 loops on right front.

Warm winter shrug

Create a casual yet elegant shrug with a lacy, open crochet stitch

Crocheted in a pattern stitch that is both lacy and substantial, this stylish piece can be paired with jeans or a long flowing skirt. Knit ribbing adds a tailored touch to the bottom and sleeve cuffs, and a delicate picot edging around the neck echoes the softness of the pattern stitch.

The shrug is worked in two identical pieces. Work each side from the cuff to the neck, and seam the halves together at the center back. Underarm and side seams are sewn next, with ribbings and neck edgings added last.

Sizing
Finished size: 40 (44, 48) in./ 1 (1.1, 1.2) m at chest; larger sizes in parentheses

Gauge
Crochet: 3 pattern repeats/ 3¼ in. (8.3cm) in pattern stitch
Knit: 20 stitches/4 in. (10cm) in k 2, p 2 ribbing, slightly stretched

Materials
- **4 (5, 6)** skeins worsted-weight yarn (Wool-Ease, Lion Brand Yarn Company, 197 yards per skein, Denim Twist #194)
- crochet hook, size J (6mm) or size needed to obtain gauge
- 16-in. (41cm) and 24-in. (61cm) circular knitting needles, size 6 (4mm) or size needed to obtain gauge
- key charm (Victorian Key, Antique Brass, JHB International, Inc., # 09045)
- 2½ yds. (2.3m) satin cord or ¼-in. (6mm) wide ribbon
- tapestry or yarn needle
- tape measure
- yarn cutter
- sewing thread and needle

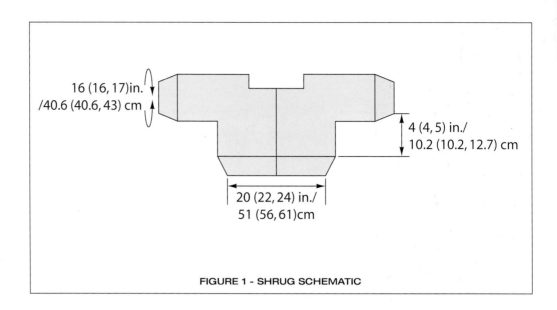

16 (16, 17)in.
/40.6 (40.6, 43) cm

4 (4, 5) in./
10.2 (10.2, 12.7) cm

20 (22, 24) in./
51 (56, 61)cm

FIGURE 1 - SHRUG SCHEMATIC

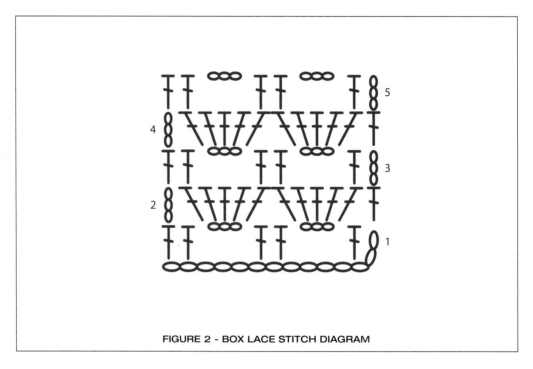

5

4

3

2

1

FIGURE 2 - BOX LACE STITCH DIAGRAM

Crochet Pattern Stitch

The crochet pattern stitch is worked over a multiple of 5 stitches plus 2 (add 2 for base chain):
*Row 1: Skip 3 ch (count as 1 dc), 1 dc into next ch, * ch 3, skip 3 ch, 1 dc into each of next 2 ch; repeat from * across, turn.*
*Row 2: Ch 3 (counts as 1dc), skip first stitch, * 5 dc into next ch 3 space; repeat from * across, ending 1 dc into top of turning ch, turn.*
*Row 3: Ch 3 (counts as 1 dc), skip first stitch, 1 dc into next dc, *ch 3, skip 3 dc, 1 dc into each of next 2 dc; repeat from * to end, turn. Repeat rows 2 and 3 for pattern (see Figure 2).*

Crochet the shrug halves

1 With crochet hook, ch 77 (77, 82).
Row 1: Skip 3 ch (count as 1 dc), 1 dc into next ch, * ch 3, skip 3 ch, 1 dc into each of next 2 ch; repeat from * across, turn.
Row 2: Ch 3 (counts as 1 dc), skip first stitch, * 5 dc into next ch 3 space; repeat from * across, ending 1 dc into top of turning ch, turn.
Row 3: Ch 3 (counts as 1 dc), skip first stitch, 1 dc into next dc, *ch 3, skip 3 dc, 1 dc into each of next 2 dc; repeat from * to end, turn.
2 Repeat rows 2 and 3 until piece measures 8 (8, 9) in./20 (20, 23) cm ending with row 2.
3 Work back/front increases:
Ch 22 (22, 27), skip 3 ch and work row 3 pattern across.

The cuff, at left, is knit 2 purl 2 ribbing. Crocheted box lace comprises the bodice and sleeves (right).

Ch 22 (22, 27), skip 3 ch and work row 2 pattern across (23, 23, 26 repeats).
4 Work even to 13 (13½, 14) in./33 (34, 35.5) cm.
5 On next row 2 of pattern, shape neck opening: Work in pattern across 52 (52, 60) stitches, sl st across center 17 stitches, ch 3, continue in pattern across to end.
6 Working sides separately and keeping neck divide, work until sides measure 17 (17, 18) in./43 (43, 46) cm from beginning. Fasten off.
7 Make a second piece to match the first. Shaping is symmetrical, so there is no need to reverse (see figure 1).
8 Hold two halves of shrug together, with last rows worked on center back abutting. Sc together to form center back seam. Sew, or single crochet, underarm and side seams.

Knit the sleeve ribbing
1 With 16-in. (41cm) circular knitting needle, pick up 78 (78, 82) stitches around one sleeve bottom.
2 Work circular k 2, p 2 ribbing for 4 in. (10cm). BO in rib.
3 Repeat steps 1–2 on the second sleeve.

Knit the bottom ribbing
1 With 24 in. (61cm) circular knitting needle, pick up 120 (136, 144) stitches along bottom edge.
2 Work k 2, p 2 ribbing for 4 in. (10cm). BO in rib.

Crochet the edging
With right side facing and working one sc in each crochet stitch around, attach yarn to lower edge of front, ch 1, *5 sc, in next stitch (1 sc, 3 ch, 1 sc, picot made); repeat from * around, ending at other lower front edge. Fasten off and work all ends in.

Finish the shrug
Using ch 3 loops, lace cord or ribbon up front opening to level desired. Thread key charm on lacing and knot ends to finish.

CREATIVE OPTIONS

Thread a ribbon or length of crochet chain through the open spaces at the bottom of the bodice and the sleeves, just above the ribbings.

Work the ribbings and edging in a contrasting color for a bolder look.

Yarn is dyed in batches, or dye lots; the colors can vary between lots. Be sure to buy enough yarn from the same dye lot to finish your project (check the labels for the dye lot number).

Victorian capelet

Create a charming overlay collar for a simple, stylish knit capelet

Work this Victorian-inspired capelet in stockinette stitch, for a soft and smooth fabric. Add garter stitch borders to prevent the inevitable curling that occurs at the edges of stockinette; this also adds a nice detail.

The lace collar overlay is a crochet edging pattern. Working this pattern in yarn on a larger hook, instead of using the traditional crochet thread and a smaller hook, creates an unusual look. For further distinction, add a ribbon or cord accent along the top.

Sizing
Finished size: 40 (47, 56) in./1 (1.2, 1.4) m at bottom

Gauge
Knit: 18 stitches/4 in. (10cm) on size 8 (5mm) needles
Crochet: Edging depth 3½ in. (8.9cm)

Materials
- **2 (2, 3)** skeins worsted-weight yarn, main color (Wool-Ease, Lion Brand Yarn Company, 197 yards per skein, Dark Rose Heather #139)
- **2** skeins worsted-weight yarn, accent color (Wool-Ease, Lion Brand, 197 yards per skein, Mink Brown #127)
- circular knitting needles, size 8 (5mm) or size needed to obtain gauge in stockinette stitch
- crochet hook, size H (5mm) or size needed to obtain gauge over edging pattern stitch
- vintage clasp (Antique Brass, JHB International, Inc., #09049)
- 1½ yds. (1.4m) ¼-in. (6mm) wide ribbon
- tapestry or yarn needle
- tape measure
- scissors
- sewing thread and needle

Crochet Pattern Stitch

Edging pattern stitch is worked over a multiple of eight stitches plus three:

Row 1: Work 1 dc into 4th chain from hook, 1 dc in each ch to end, turn.

Row 2: Ch 3, 1 dc in each dc across, turn.

*Row 3: Ch 1, 1 sc into each of first 3 dc, * 2 ch, skip 1 dc, into next dc work (2 dc, 2 ch) twice, skip 1 dc, 1 sc into each of next 5 dc; repeat from * to end omitting 2 sc at end of last repeat and working last sc into top of 3 ch at beg of previous row, turn.*

*Row 4: Ch 1, 1 sc into each of first 2 sc, *3 ch, skip next 2 ch space, into next 2 ch space work (3 dc, ch 2, 3 dc), ch 3, skip 1 sc, 1sc into each of next 3 sc; repeat from * to end omitting 1 sc at end of last repeat, turn.*

*Row 5: 1 ch, 1 sc into first sc, *4 ch, skip next 3 ch space, into next 2ch space work (4 dc, 2 ch, 4 dc), 4 ch, skip 1 sc, 1 sc into next sc; repeat from * to end, turn.*

*Row 6: Ch 1, 1 sc into first sc, *6 ch, skip next 4 ch space, into next ch 2 space work (4 dc, 2 ch, 4 dc), 6 ch, 1 sc into next sc; repeat from * to end, turn.*

*Row 7: Ch 1, *6 sc in 6 ch space, 1sc in each dc, into next ch 2 space work (sc, ch 3, sc), sc in each dc, 6 sc in 6ch space, skip 1 sc; repeat from * across, end sc in last sc, end off (see Figure 2).*

Technique Note:

Work increase rows on right side. To avoid unsightly holes, work the increases by picking up the "bar" from the row below and knitting it through the back loop (make one). See Basics chapter for more information.

Knit the capelet

1 With knitting needles and MC, CO 107 (123, 147) stitches.

2 K 5 stitches and place marker, k to last five stitches, and place marker. Keep these stitches in garter stitch for entire piece.

3 K 5, P to last five stitches, k 5. Keeping first and last 5 stitches in garter stitch, work in stockinette stitch until piece measures 4 in. (10cm). End with a wrong-side row.

4 Work increase row: Keeping 5 edge stitches in garter stitch, k 2, M1 across body stitches (139, 161, 193 stitches).

5 Work even until piece measures 8 in. (20cm).

6 Work increase row as above (182, 211, 254 stitches).

7 Work even until piece measures 11¼ in. (28.5cm).

8 Work five rows in garter stitch. BO and work in all ends (see Figure 1).

Crochet the lace collar overlay

1 With right side of capelet facing, use accent yarn and crochet hook to attach yarn to neck edge. Ch 1, sc in each knit stitch across, ch 3, turn.

Row 1: Work 1 dc into each dc across, turn.

Row 2: Ch 3, 1 dc in each dc across, turn.

Row 3: Ch 1, 1 sc into each of first 3 dc, * ch 2, skip 1 dc, into next dc work (2 dc, ch 2) twice, skip 1 dc, 1 sc into each of next 5 dc; repeat from * to end omitting 2 sc at end of last repeat and working last sc into top of 3 ch at beg of previous row, turn.

Row 4: Ch 1, 1 sc into each of first 2 sc, *ch 3, skip next 2 ch space, into next 2 ch space work (3 dc, ch 2, 3 dc),

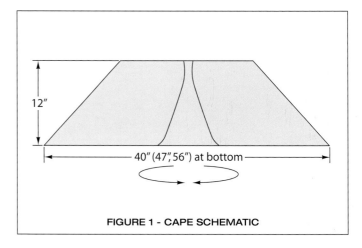

FIGURE 1 - CAPE SCHEMATIC

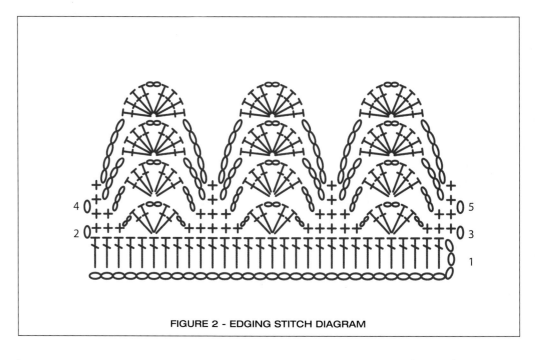

FIGURE 2 - EDGING STITCH DIAGRAM

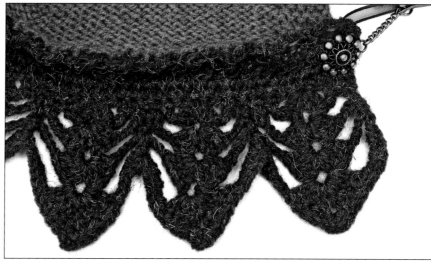

The edges of the capelet are worked in garter stitch. The collar overlay is crocheted Gothic lace.

3 ch, skip 1 sc, 1 sc into each of next 3 sc; repeat from * to end omitting 1 sc at end of last repeat, turn.

Row 5: Ch 1, 1 sc into first sc, *4 ch, skip next 3 ch space, into next 2 ch space work (4 dc, ch 2, 4 dc), ch 4, skip 1 sc, 1 sc into next sc; repeat from * to end, turn.

Row 6: Ch 1, 1 sc into first sc, *ch 6, skip next 4 ch space, into next 2ch space work (4 dc, ch 2, 4 dc), ch 6, 1 sc into next sc; repeat from * to end, turn.

Row 7: Ch 1, *6 sc in 6 ch space, 1 sc in each dc, into next ch 2 space work (sc, ch 3, sc), sc in each dc, 6 sc in

6 ch space, skip 1 sc; repeat from * across, end sc in last sc, end off. Work ends in.

2 Fold collar down over capelet. With wrong side facing, attach accent yarn to neck edge, ch 4.

3 Working along folded edge, * ch 2, skip 2 stitches, 1 hdc, repeat from * across, end with 1 hdc in last stitch. Fasten off and work in ends.

Finish the capelet

1 Thread ribbon or cording through beading at neck.
2 Attach closure to neck and front.

CREATIVE OPTIONS

Try different combinations of yarn colors for other looks. Go casual with a bright color over black or add drama with black and white.

Attach beads or small tassels to each edging point.

Attach a large silk flower to a pin to close the neckline for a feminine look.

When yarn label instructions say "dry flat," you will need a large, moisture-resistant surface such as a sweater-drying screen. It's okay to place smaller items on a solid surface, but turn them frequently to dry both sides.

Field of flowers cardigan

Create an openwork cardigan with the look of heavy vintage lace

Work the body of this cardigan sweater in two separate crochet motifs, and join them on the last round. Knit the sleeves in stockinette stitch for less bulk and more coverage; the solid sleeve fabric contrasts nicely with the openwork bodice.

Sizing
Finished Size: 39 (52) in./99cm (1.3m) at chest; larger size in parentheses

Gauge
Knit: 16 stitches/4 in. (10cm) over stockinette stitch with larger needles
Crochet: Motif 1 is 3¼ in. (8.2cm) in diameter at the widest part, and Motif 2 is 1¼ in. (3.2cm) across.

Materials
- **9 (12)** skeins light worsted or double-knit yarn (Microspun, Lion Brand Yarn Company, 168 yards per skein: Lily White #100)
- straight knitting needles, sizes 6 (4mm) and 8 (5mm) or size needed to obtain gauge
- crochet hook, size F (3.75mm) or size needed to obtain gauge
- **5** porcelain buttons (China Rose Porcelain buttons, JHB International, Inc., #32642)
- tapestry or yarn needle
- tape measure
- yarn cutter
- sewing thread and needle

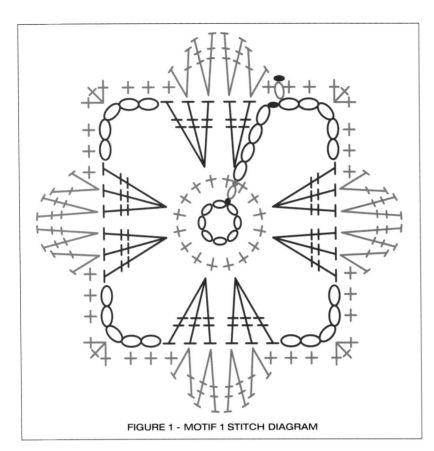

FIGURE 1 - MOTIF 1 STITCH DIAGRAM

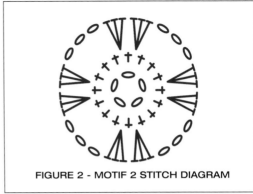

FIGURE 2 - MOTIF 2 STITCH DIAGRAM

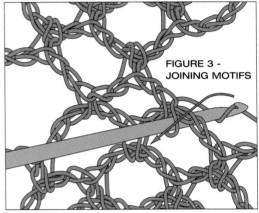

FIGURE 3 - JOINING MOTIFS

CREATIVE OPTIONS

Use multiple colors, brights, or pastels for the motifs.

Choose a contrasting color for the sleeves.

Fasten your cardigan with unusual closures for a personal touch. Try toggles or woven frogs.

Make a coordinating neck or waist scarf: With size 8 (5mm) needles, CO 18 stitches and work in seed stitch until scarf is desired length. BO and work in ends.

Crochet Motif 1

Ch 8, slip stitch into first ch to form a ring.
Round 1: *Ch 1, work 16 sc into ring, sl st into first sc.*
Round 2: *Ch 4 (counts as 1 tr), 2 tr into first sc, 3 tr into next sc, ch 5, (skip 2 sc, 3 tr into each of next 2 sc, ch 5) 3 times, sl st into 4th ch at beginning of round.*
Round 3: *Ch 1, 1 sc into same stitch as sl st, *(1 hdc, 1 dc) into next tr, 2 tr into each of next 2 tr (join between these 2 tr groups), (1 dc, 1 hdc) into next tr, 1 sc into next tr, 1 sc into each of next 2 ch, 3 sc in next ch, 1 sc into each of next 2 ch, 1 sc into next tr; repeat from * 3 times more omitting 1 sc at end of last repeat, sl st into first sc. Fasten off (see Figure 1).*

Crochet Motif 2

Ch 5, slip stitch into first ch to form a ring
Round 1: *Ch 1, work 16 sc into ring, slip stitch into first sc.*
Round 2: *Ch 2 (Counts as 1 hdc), 2 hdc into first sc, 3 hdc into next sc, ch 3, (skip 2 sc, 3 hdc into each of next 2 sc, ch 3) 3 times, slip stitch into 3rd ch at beginning of round. Fasten off (see Figure 2).*

Technique Notes

You will be joining the first motifs (Motif 1) to each other as you make them. This is worked in Round 3 between the 2 tr groups as noted in the round. Simply sl st into the corresponding space of the previous motif(s) to join. Then complete the current unit as written.
The second units (Motif 2) will be joined into the spaces left between the first motifs in a similar manner. This join is worked on the second ch of the ch 3 spaces. Slip stitch into the middle sc of the ch 5 space of the surrounding units (see Figure 3).

Crochet the cardigan back

1 Make first Motif 1 as described above. Work in yarn ends.
2 Make second Motif 1 and join in third round as noted above to one side of first motif.
3 Continue to make and join units as shown in Figure 4. Make 42 (56) Motif 1s for back.
4 Make Motif 2 and join as described above. Continue to make and join units as shown in assembly diagram. Make 30 (42) Motif 2s for back, plus four (six) more for joining side and shoulders.

Crochet the cardigan fronts

1 As with back, make first Motif 1 as described. Work in yarn ends.

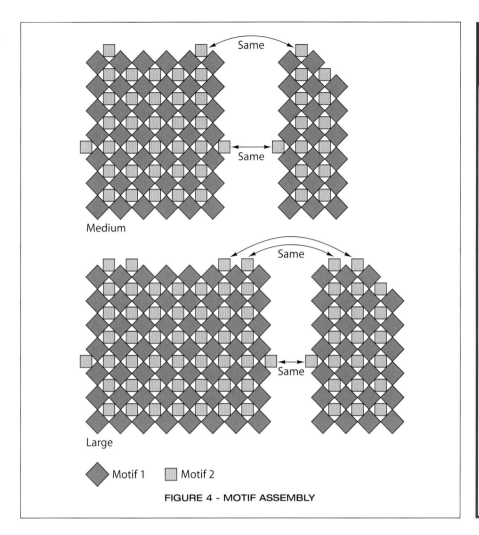

Medium

Large

◆ Motif 1   ▨ Motif 2

FIGURE 4 - MOTIF ASSEMBLY

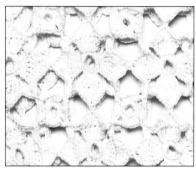
2 Make second Motif 1 and join in third round as noted above to one side of first motif. Continue to make and join units as shown in Figure 4. Make 20 (27) motifs for one front.

3 Make Motif 2 and join as discussed above. Continue to make and join units as shown in assembly diagram. Make 12 (18) Motif 2s for one front.

4 Repeat steps 1–3 to make second front, but reverse shaping by placing neck edge on other side as in Figure 4.

Side and shoulder seams

1 Connect shoulder Motifs 1 and 2 in a similar manner to close shoulder seams following assembly diagram.

2 Join 4th and 5th motifs from top on each side to make side seams. The lower two units are left free to form side slits (see Figure 4).

Knit the sleeves

(worked from cuff to shoulder)

1 With smaller needles, CO 58 (60).

2 Work k 1, p 1 ribbing for 1 in. (2.5cm).

3 Switch to larger needles and begin working in stockinette stitch.

4 Begin sleeve increases:
Inc 1 stitch at each end of right side rows every other row to 98 (98) stitches.

5 Work even to 9 (9½) in./23 (24) cm. BO all stitches. Work ends in.

6 Repeat steps 1–5 to make a second sleeve.

Finish the cardigan

1 Sew sleeve underarm seams.

2 Attach yarn to sleeve upper edge at underarm seam, ch 1. Begin working sc across sleeve top. At the same time, attach sleeve into armhole by slip stitching into join locations of each motif across.

3 Attach buttons to edge of motifs on left front to correspond to spaces between 2 tr groups. These spaces will function as buttonholes.

Jaunty jacket

Warm and comfortable – perfect for a walk in the country or a snuggle at home

This jacket will take more than an evening to make, but it is definitely worth the time. The soft, thick yarn and subtle color patterning create a winning combination.

Work the body from the top down, using a crochet stitch from a group of stitches known as griddle stitches. These stitches, paired with soft, lofty yarn, result in a wonderfully warm, textured jacket.

To contrast, work the sleeves and hood in stockinette stitch with a smooth, lighter-weight yarn. Ribbed cuffs and a ribbed front border complete the knit portions of the jacket.

Sizing
Finished size: 39 (44, 49) in./ 1 (1.1, 1.2) m at chest; larger sizes in parentheses

Gauge
Crochet: 12 stitches/5 in. (13cm) in pattern stitch
Knit: 16 stitches/4 in. (10cm) over stockinette stitch with larger needle

Materials
- **4 (4, 5)** skeins bulky yarn, main color (Homespun, Lion Brand Yarn Company, 185 yards per skein, Nouveau #338)
- **3 (4, 4)** skeins worsted-weight yarn, accent color (Wool-Ease, Lion Brand Yarn Company, 197 yards per skein: Mink Brown #127)
- crochet hook, size N or size needed to obtain gauge
- 24-in. (61cm) or longer circular knitting needles, size 8 (5mm) or size needed to obtain gauge
- straight knitting needles, size 9 (5.5mm) or size needed to obtain gauge
- tapestry or yarn needle
- tape measure
- yarn cutter

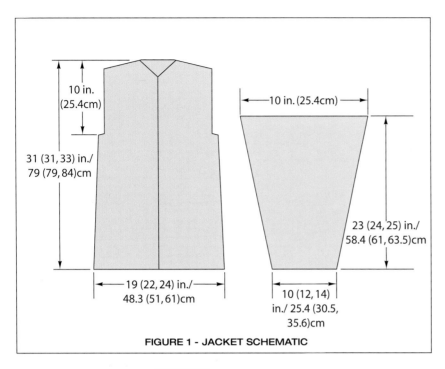

FIGURE 1 - JACKET SCHEMATIC

10 in.
(25.4cm)

31 (31, 33) in./
79 (79, 84)cm

19 (22, 24) in./
48.3 (51, 61)cm

10 in. (25.4cm)

23 (24, 25) in./
58.4 (61, 63.5)cm

10 (12, 14)
in./ 25.4 (30.5,
35.6)cm

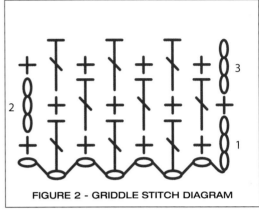

FIGURE 2 - GRIDDLE STITCH DIAGRAM

Crochet Pattern Stitch

The pattern stitch is worked over a multiple of 2 stitches plus 1:
Ch desired length, multiple of 2 plus 1
Row 1: *Skip 3 ch (count as 1 dc), * 1 sc into next ch, 1 dc into next ch, repeat from * to end, turn.*
Row 2: *Ch 3 (counts as 1 dc), skip first stitch, * 1 sc in next dc, 1 dc in next sc, repeat from * across row, ending with last dc in top of turning ch, turn.*
Repeat row 2 for pattern (see Figure 2).

Crochet the jacket back

1 With MC yarn, ch 41 (48, 55) stitches.
Row 1: Skip 3 ch (count as 1 dc), * 1 sc into next ch, 1 dc into next ch, repeat from * to end of chain, turn.
Row 2: Ch 3 (counts as 1 dc), skip first stitch, * 1 sc in next dc, 1 dc in next sc, repeat from * across row, ending with last dc in top of turning ch, turn.
2 Repeat row 2 until piece measures 10 in. (25cm) from beginning.
3 Armhole increase row: Inc 2 stitches at each end, keeping in pattern (45, 52, 59 stitches).
4 Work even until piece measures 20 in. (51cm).
5 Increase rows: Inc 1 stitch at each end of next 2 rows (49, 56, 63 stitches).
6 Work even until piece measures 31 (31, 33) in./79 (79, 84) cm or desired length. Fasten off. Work in ends.

Crochet the fronts

1 With MC yarn, ch 12 (17, 19) stitches.
2 Work row 1 of pattern.
3 Begin row 2 of pattern and work 5 increase rows by increasing two stitches at neck edge (22, 26, 29 stitches).
4 Work even in pattern until piece measures 10 in. (25cm)

from beginning.

5 Armhole increase row: Inc 2 stitches at arm edge, keeping in pattern (24, 29, 31 stitches).
6 Work even until piece measures 20 in. (51cm).
7 Increase rows: Inc 1 stitch at each end of next 2 rows (26, 31, 33 stitches).
8 Work even until piece measures 31 (31, 33 in.) /79 (79, 84) cm or desired length. Fasten off. Work in ends.
9 Repeat steps 1–8 to make a second front. This stitch is reversible so there is no need to reverse shaping. Just turn one over to make left and right fronts.

Knit the sleeves
(worked from cuff to shoulder)
1 With smaller knitting needles and accent yarn, CO 40 (48, 56) stitches.
2 Work k 1, p 2 ribbing for 2 in. (5cm).
3 Switch to larger needles and begin working in stockinette stitch.
4 Begin sleeve increases: Inc 1 stitch at each end of right side rows every 1 in. (2.5cm) to 80 (80, 80) stitches.
5 Work even to 23 (24, 25) in./58.4 (61, 63.5) cm. BO all stitches. Work in ends (see Figure 1).

Finish the jacket
Sew all seams (shoulder, side, and sleeve underarm) and sew sleeves into armholes.

Add the hood
1 With right side of garment facing you, pick up 73 (87, 98) stitches on larger knitting needle with accent yarn.
2 Work stockinette stitch for 16 in. (41cm). BO all stitches.
3 Fold hood in half, wrong sides together, and sew top seam.

Front band
1 Using accent yarn and smaller size long circular needle, with right side of garment facing you, pick up 376 (376, 392) stitches along right front, hood and left front edges.
2 Work k 2, p 2 ribbing for 2 in. (5cm).
BO loosely and work in all ends.

> Griddle stitch, created by including short and long stitches in the same row, offers an intriguing texture and a flexible fabric.

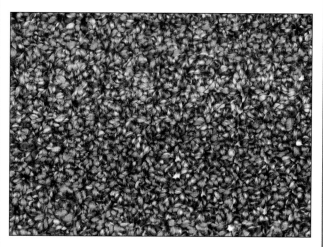
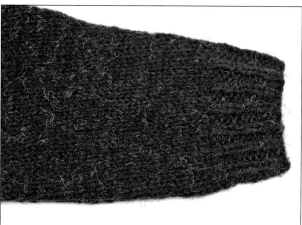

Basics

KNIT AND CROCHET BASICS

Gauge

What is it and why is it so important?

Simply put, gauge is the number of stitches and rows per inch (2.5cm), including fractions of stitches. The more essential information is that it is absolutely individual to *you*, the knitter or crocheter. No matter what the pattern and yarn wrapper say, check your gauge for every project with the needles or hook you are going to use – even if you have worked with that particular yarn before. A gauge different from that specified in a pattern will result in a finished item that is too large, or worse, too small.

Gauge depends on many things: the yarn texture and weight, the hook or needle size, the pattern stitch used, how you feel that day, and maybe even the phase of the moon. The gauge can vary even among different colors of the same yarn – it's not uncommon that black yarn can work much differently than lighter colors of the same brand and type. Gauge also can be influenced by the material a needle or hook is made of: You may obtain a slightly different gauge using aluminum tools than you would with wood or plastic. Gauge is affected by yarn substitutions, as well, since a different yarn may not work to the same gauge as one specified in a pattern. (That doesn't mean that you can't substitute yarns, but you must work a gauge swatch and adjust your hook or needle size accordingly.)

To work a gauge swatch, knit or crochet a 4-in. (10cm) square in the pattern stitch specified, using the yarn and tools noted in the pattern. Count the stitches and rows in a 2-in. (5cm) square section of the swatch. Be sure to count fractions of stitches if they exist; they can make a significant difference in the finished item. Multiply your stitch and row count by two and compare your gauge to that in the pattern for a 4-in. swatch. If you have fewer stitches than the pattern requires, switch to a smaller hook or needles and work another gauge swatch. If your work has more stitches, try a larger hook or needle.

Sizing

The patterns in this book are designed to flatter a range of figures, and most are offered in small, medium, and large sizes. The smallest size comes first, with larger sizes following in parentheses. Be sure to note where the pattern specifies finished sizes of the garment: This is the actual measurement of the garment.

Ease refers to the amount of extra room you have when you wear the garment – that is, how much bigger the clothing is than you are. Determine the amount of ease by subtracting your actual body measurement from the finished garment measurement.

All of these designs have been adjusted for the correct amount of ease according to standard sizing charts. However, please compare your measurements to the finished garment and choose a size down if you prefer a more fitted garment or a size up if you prefer more ease. Keep in mind that a garment with no ease (that is, it measures the same as your body measurements), will be extremely form-fitting. Generally, 2-4 in. (5-10cm) of ease is much more flattering and comfortable.

Yarn quantities

While every effort has been made to insure the quantities of yarn specified in the materials lists are adequate to make the projects, please keep in mind that every knitter and crocheter is different and may require more or less yarn. Also, any changes to the pattern (in length, or additions of Creative Options) may require adjustments to the amounts of yarn used. Please use your judgment in these situations. I recommend purchasing a little extra yarn (check to be sure that the dye lots are all the same). Most of the knitters and crocheters I know are usually happy to have extra yarn for a rainy day.

YARN WEIGHTS

Yarn is often referred to by weight. This is not necessarily a reference to how much the yarn actually weighs; it is a classification system to sort the yarns into categories based on how thick or thin they are. Each weight category of yarn generally corresponds to a particular range of stitch gauges and needle sizes to yield a pleasing fabric.

The confusing part is that different countries, even different needleworkers, may have different terms for the same weight of yarn. The table shows some terms commonly used to refer to yarn weights and the average number of stockinette or single crochet stitches over 4 in. (10cm). This information is taken from the Craft Yarn Council of America's yarn standards Web site (yarnstandards.com).

When choosing a pattern, pay attention to the weight of yarn specified. A thicker yarn makes a project progress quickly, because there are fewer stitches per inch and row to be worked. Thicker yarns often produce a much warmer fabric than thinner yarns because of their loft. This loft also helps them produce a hefty, bulky fabric.

A thinner yarn may not have the insulating loft of a bulky yarn, but it may produce a lighter, more manageable fabric.

Another consideration is ply. Ply means strand and refers to the number of threads that have been twisted together to make up the finished yarn. Count the number of plies in most yarns by untwisting the end. This does not apply to some novelty yarns, as they are just one strand. The weight of the plied yarn is not necessarily related to the number of plies, but it is related to the thickness of the individual strands.

The projects in this book have been designed with the different

Weight	Type	Knit Gauge	Crochet Gauge
Superfine	Sock Fingering Baby	27-32 stitches	21-32 stitches
Fine	Sport Baby	23-26 stitches	16-20 stitches
Light	DK Light Worsted	21-24 stitches	12-17 stitches
Medium	Worsted Afghan Aran	16-20 stitches	11-14 stitches
Bulky	Chunky Craft Rug	12-15 stitches	8-11 stitches
Super Bulky	Bulky Roving	6-11 stitches	5-9 stitches

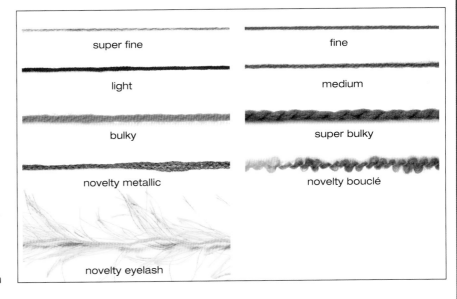

super fine

fine

light

medium

bulky

super bulky

novelty metallic

novelty bouclé

novelty eyelash

yarn weights and their attributes in mind. The body of the jacket on p. 70 is worked in a soft, bulky yarn to provide warmth. The jacket sleeves are made in a medium, or worsted, weight yarn for less bulk and better movement.

Many of these projects, including the shrug on p. 58 and the skirt on p. 50, use medium-weight yarns. In addition to creating a flattering, comfortable fabric, medium-weight yarns also offer a reasonable completion time.

Sometimes only a finer yarn, such as the yarns used in the shrug on p. 54 and the cardigan on p. 66, will do. A light worsted or DK yarn works well for soft, feminine projects.

ENGLISH METHOD

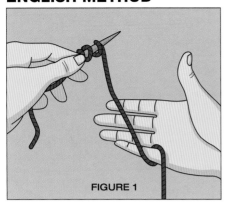

FIGURE 1

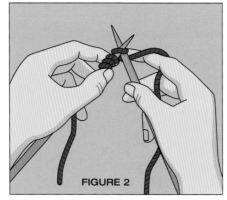

FIGURE 2

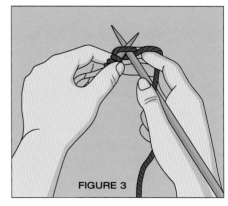

FIGURE 3

KNITTING

Holding the yarn and needles

There are about as many different ways to hold yarn and knitting needles as there are people who knit. The most important thing is that you are comfortable and able to produce a result that satisfies you. The way you hold your yarn and needles will be a product of how you choose, or have learned, to knit.

The two basic methods of holding the work are the English method (**Figures 1–3**) and the Continental method (**Figures 4–5**). In the English method, you hold the working, or ball, yarn in your right hand. With the Continental method, the working yarn is held in your left hand. If you try one method but have trouble getting comfortable with your knitting or regulating the tension on the stitches, you might like to try the other method to see if it suits you better.

CONTINENTAL METHOD

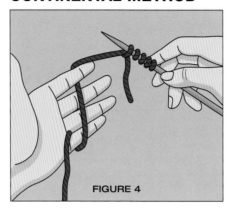

FIGURE 4

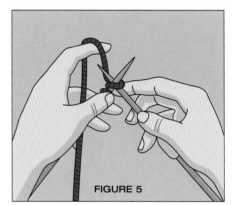

FIGURE 5

Because the Continental method of holding the working yarn is similar to that used in crochet, you may find it much easier to master if you learned to crochet before learning to knit. In my own experience, I did not really begin to enjoy knitting until I switched to the Continental method. Because of my previous crochet experience, it seemed a more natural way to hold and control the yarn.

If you find you have dropped a stitch when knitting, don't panic! To solve the problem, work to just above the dropped stitch and use a crochet hook to "hook" the stitch back up the ladder left when it ran down. Be sure to note which side is a knit and which is a purl and hook accordingly.

Casting on

There are quite a few different methods of casting on, and most knitters have their favorite. The one common thing among them is that you must first cast on to begin to knit.

The first cast-on stitch is one that many knitters use and is among the easiest to master. It is often referred to as "knitting on," as it is almost identical to the knit stitch itself. The second method presented is very similar but produces a much more attractive and sturdy edge. It is among my favorite cast-on methods and is often called "cable cast-on." Give them both a try and see which you prefer.

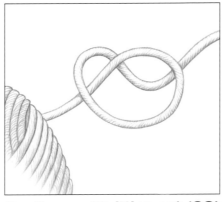

Casting on (Knitting on) (CO)
1 Pull the yarn end from the center of the skein and make a loop, leaving a 6-in. (15cm) tail.

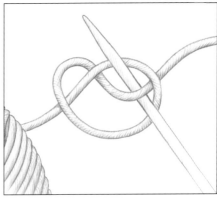

2 Insert the needle into the loop as shown. Tighten the loop around your needle. This counts as your first stitch.

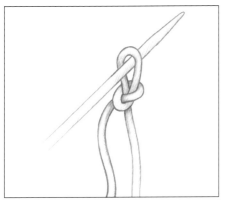

3 Hold the needle with the first stitch in your left hand, keeping the tail in front of the needle and the yarn from the skein in back of the needle.

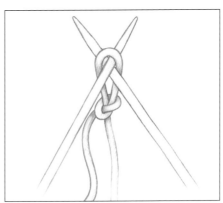

4 Hold the empty needle in your right hand and slide its tip through the stitch on the left needle from left to right (from the front of the stitch to the back). The needles will form an X, with the right needle behind the left needle.

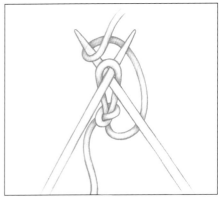

5 Hold the crossed needles between your left thumb and forefinger. Using your right hand, wrap the yarn from the skein counterclockwise around the tip of the right needle. Pull the tip of the right needle down and through the stitch, pulling the new loop through.

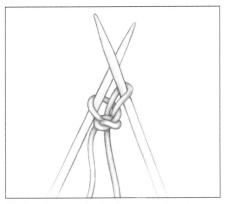

6 Gently stretch the loop on the right needle.

7 Working from left to right, slide the tip of the left needle through the loop on the right needle as shown.

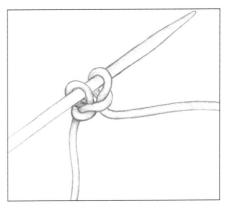

8 Slide the right needle out of the loop, leaving two loops on the left needle. Pull gently to tighten the second stitch. Slide the tip of the right needle into the top stitch.

Repeat steps 5–8 until you have cast on the required number of stitches.

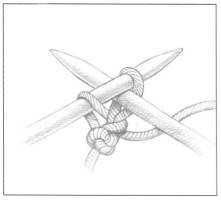

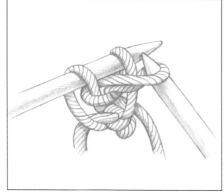

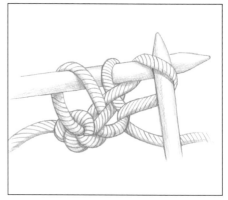

Casting on (Cable cast-on) (CO)

Follow steps 1 through 8 of the knitting-on cast-on once. You now have two stitches on the left needle.

1 Insert the right needle between the two stitches on the left needle, as shown.

2 Wrap the yarn from the skein counterclockwise around the tip of the right needle. Pull the tip of the right needle down and through the stitch, pulling the new loop through. Gently stretch the loop on the right needle.

3 Place the new stitch on the left needle as shown. Repeat steps 1–3 until you have cast on the required number of stitches.

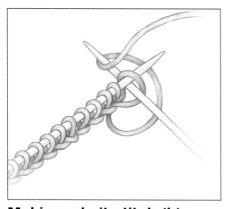

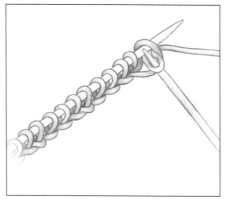

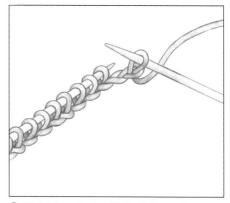

Making a knit stitch (k)

1 Hold the needle with the cast-on stitches in your left hand, with the first stitch (the last cast-on stitch) about 1 in. (2.5cm) from the needle tip. Slide the tip of the right needle into the first stitch, forming an X with the needles. Wrap the yarn from the skein counterclockwise around the tip of the right needle.

2 Slide the right needle and its loop down through the middle of the stitch.

3 Slide the stitch off the left needle, leaving the loop on the right needle. Repeat steps 1–3 until all of the stitches have been knit off the left needle; this completes your first row. Switch the empty needle to your right hand and the full one to your left hand and continue working rows.

Ball, skein, or hank? Balls are just what you think – yarn wound into a shape resembling a ball. The yarn is worked from the outside. Skeins are bundles and often have an end sticking out so you can work from the center. Hanks are just loose circles of yarn, twisted up into a little package.

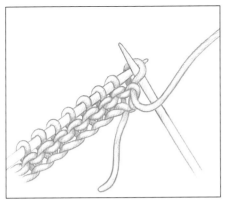

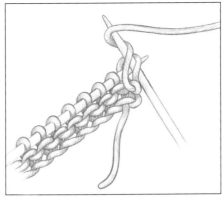

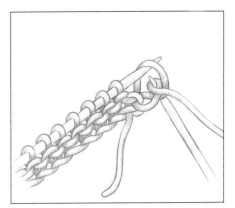

Making a purl stitch (p)

1 With the yarn in front of the left needle, slide the tip of the right needle from right to left through the first stitch. The needles will form an X, with the right needle in front.

2 Wrap the yarn counterclockwise around the tip of the right needle.

3 Slide the right needle from front to back through the center of the stitch.

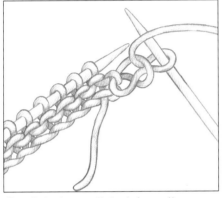

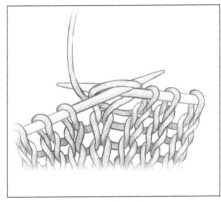

4 Pull the loop off the left needle, leaving the loop on the right needle. Continue until the desired number of purl stitches are made.

Increasing (inc)

Increasing means adding more stitches to a row. There are many different types of increases; some are more visible than others. Here are two methods that are used in the projects in this book. The first, a visible increase, is called a *bar increase* because a horizontal bar will follow the increased stitch on the knit side. The second is a *make one increase* – this type is nearly invisible, and is made by lifting a loop up from the previous row.

Bar increase (inc)

1 To add a knit stitch, slide the right needle into the stitch, wrap the yarn around the needle, and pull the loop down through the middle of the stitch. Do not drop the stitch off the left needle.

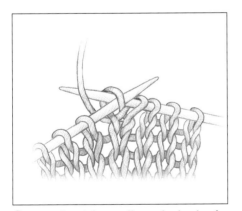

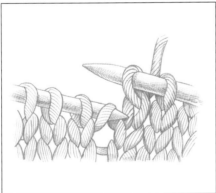

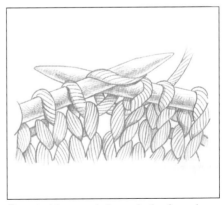

2 Bring the right needle to the back of the loop and knit into it, dropping the loop off the needle when finished.

Make one (inc)

1 Insert the left needle from back to front into the horizontal strand in the row below. It is between the stitches you are currently working.

2 Knit this strand through the front loop to twist the stitch. If it is not twisted, a hole will appear in your work.

Decreasing (dec)

Decreasing means reducing the number of stitches in a row. As with increases, there are quite a few different types of decreases. Generally, your pattern will specify the type to be used. If not, here the simplest method is to knit or purl two stitches together (K2tog or P2tog).

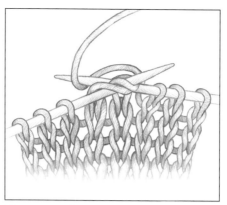

Decreasing (dec)

Insert the right needle from front to back through two stitches on the left needle and knit the stitches together. Or, insert the right needle from back to front through two stitches and purl together.

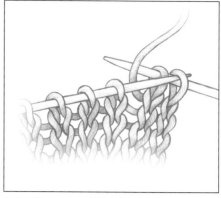

Binding off (BO)

To bind off, place the full needle in your left hand and the empty needle in your right hand and knit two stitches onto the right needle.

1 Slide the tip of the left needle into the first or outer stitch, pull it up and over the second or inner stitch, and drop it off the needle.

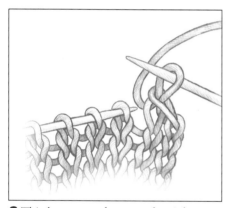

2 This leaves one loop on the right needle. To continue, knit another stitch onto the right needle and repeat step 1.

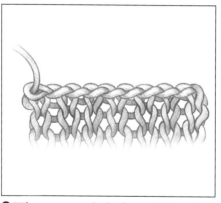

3 When you reach the last stitch on the left needle, knit it onto the right needle and repeat step 1. One loop remains on the needle. Cut the yarn, remove the loop, pass the yarn through the loop, and tighten.

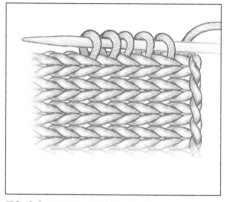

Picking up stitches

To pick up stitches from the side of a piece, slide your right needle between the bars along the side of the edge, wrap the yarn around the needle, and pull it through. Continue, spacing stitches evenly, until you have picked up the required amount of stitches.

Alternatively, you can use a crochet hook to pull the loops through before placing them on the needle.

Weaving in ends

Once all stitches have been bound off, the yarn ends should be woven in for a neat finish. Thread each yarn tail through a tapestry needle and weave it in and out of stitches on the wrong side of the fabric to secure. Be careful not to pull so tightly that the fabric puckers. Trim the excess yarn when finished.

Knitting Practice —
Practice knitting in the round and make a scarf tube – a scarf with no wrong side and a multitude of uses. Cast on 100 to 150 stitches, join, and work in the round in the stitch of your choice until you're out of yarn or you just can't stand it anymore; bind off. The resulting tube is a wonderfully warm scarf with a built-in hat at either end.

USING CIRCULAR NEEDLES

Circular knitting needles have several advantages, in addition to enabling you to work in the round. Use them to knit flat, instead of using straight needles; just turn the work at the end of the row. This shifts the weight of the knitting to your lap, reducing the strain on your hands. Circular needles also are more portable. They never leave the knitting, so you won't lose a needle, and they tuck away more neatly than long straight needles.

Circular needles come in a range of lengths, starting with 11½-in. (29cm) long needles designed for very small areas, such as socks or cuffs. (In some cases, they are so awkward that using double-pointed needles may be easier.) Longer lengths include 16 in. (41cm), 24 in. (61cm), 29 in. (73.6cm), and 36 in. (.9m). Some manufacturers even produce 60-in. (1.5m) circulars.

When choosing a circular needle, be sure to select the shortest length that will comfortably hold all the stitches. Too long a needle is just as frustrating as too short.

Knitting in the round

Some of the projects in this book are knitted in the round (the cap on p. 18 and the socks on p. 34, for example). For some knitters, myself included, circular knitting is the preferred method of constructing items. When working in the round, the right side of the work is always facing you, so you only work right-side rows. In stockinette fabric, this means always working the knit stitch. (I don't know too many knitters who prefer purling to knitting, so this is a big advantage to working in the round.) The resulting fabric is smooth stockinette, not bumpy garter stitch. This little touch of knitting magic results from the construction of knit and purl stitches themselves. In effect, you work both the right and wrong side rows at the same time. (You can work garter stitch in the round by purling every other row, as you would if working flat.)

Circular knitting also reduces, or even eliminates, the need for sewing up seams, thus making finishing much easier. Most, but not all, stitch patterns can be worked in the round, with intarsia (creating pictures) being an exception.

Knitting in the round is achieved by using either a circular needle, which is two knitting needles joined by a flexible cable, or a set of double-pointed needles. With either method, you must make absolutely sure that the cast-on row is not twisted when you join to work in the round. A twisted cast-on cannot be corrected once you have worked past the first round. You will have to rip out the work and start over, so please check carefully.

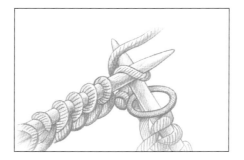

Working with circular needles

Cast on as you would normally, and distribute the stitches around the needle, being sure not to twist them.

Hold the needle with the last cast-on stitch in your right hand and the tip with the first cast on stitch in your left. (You may wish to place a stitch marker to mark the beginning of the round.) Knit the first cast-on stitch, pulling the yarn snug to avoid a gap. Continue to knit the cast-on row until you reach the beginning of the round. Double check that the work is not twisted – you can still right it at this point as a small twist in one row will not show. Continue working in the round, moving the stitch marker as needed.

Double-pointed needles

These are the original needles for working in the round, and they still work well today. The principle is the same as for working on a circular needle; it just takes some practice to get used to using more than two needles.

When using double-pointed needles, divide the stitches evenly among three or four needles (with one needle left to work the stitches). The more stitches to work, the more needles you will need.

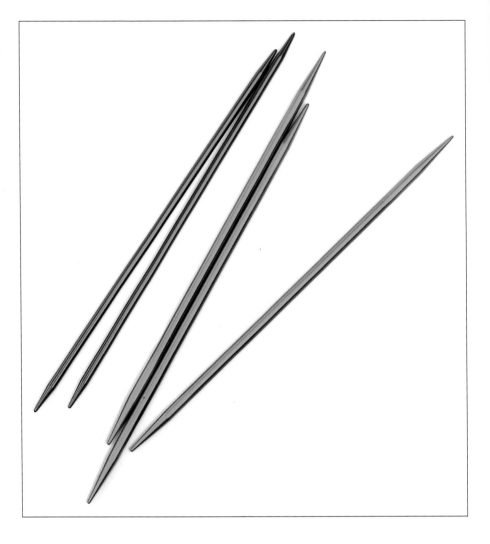

You may find it easier to use a straight needle to cast on all the stitches at one time and then transfer them to the double-pointed needles.

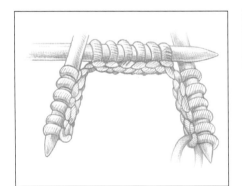

Using double-pointed needles
1 Cast on the required number of stitches.
2 Arrange the needles with the cast-on edge toward the center.

3 Hold the needle with the last cast-on stitch in your right hand and the needle with the first cast-on stitch in your left. Knit the first cast-on stitch, pulling the yarn snug to avoid a gap.

Continue to work across the first needle. When all stitches are worked off, it becomes the free needle. Using the free needle, work across the next set of stitches. Continue working in rounds in this manner.

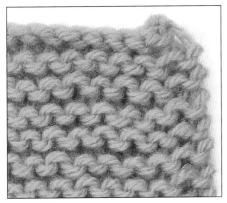

Basic knit stitch patterns

Garter stitch is formed by knitting or purling every row in flat knitting. It can also be worked by alternating knit and purl rows in the round.

Working alternate rows of knit and purl flat produces *stockinette stitch* and, on the back side, *reverse stockinette* stitch. In the round, stockinette and reverse stockinette are produced by knitting or purling every round.

Instead of alternating knit and purl every row, you can alternate them within the row to produce *ribbing*. In ribbing, knit stitches line up over other knit stitches and purls line up over purls. The number of knit and purl stitches alternated determines how the ribbing looks and fits. Knit one, purl one (k 1, p 1) ribbing is as it says: one knit stitch followed by a purl stitch across the row. This is sometimes referred to as 1 by 1 ribbing. It follows that other ribbings would be made similarly, as 2 by 2 or 3 by 5, and so on.

Seed stitch is a lovely textured stitch made by working knit and purl stitches alternated within the row, but also alternated every row so that the knit stitches do not line up over the other knit stitches every row. A good way to think about it is 1 by 1 ribbing, moved over one every row.

ACCESSORIES

There are a great many knit and crochet accessories you can acquire. Many of them are not essential, but they can be helpful and even enjoyable to find and collect. Here is a short and certainly not inclusive list:

- tape measure
- stitch gauge
- stitch marker rings
- stitch holders
- bobbins
- plastic head pins or T-pins
- point protectors (slide these over the points of knitting needles to prevent projects in progress from slipping off the needles)
- cable needles
- yarn needles (use these for sewing seams and working in ends)
- scissors
- storage and project bags

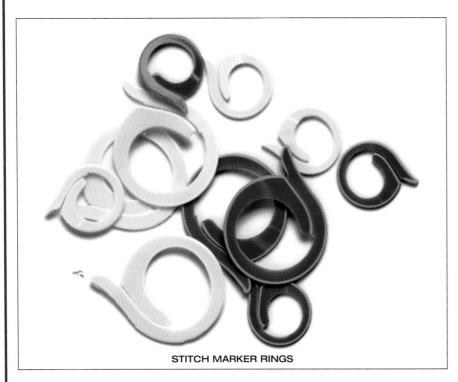

STITCH MARKER RINGS

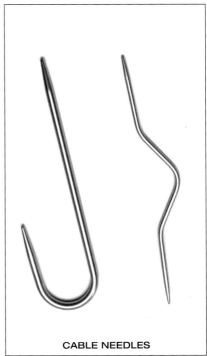

CABLE NEEDLES

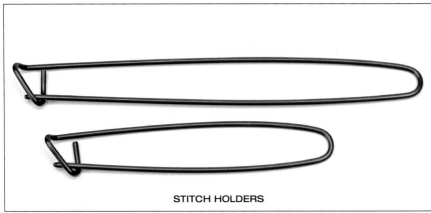

STITCH HOLDERS

POINT PROTECTORS

CROCHETING

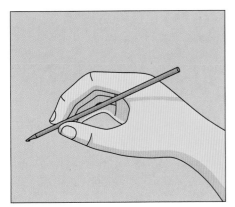

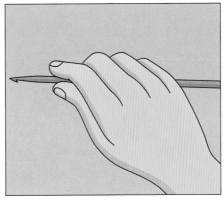

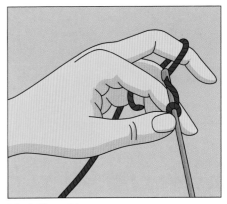

Holding the hook

There are many different ways to hold a crochet hook, but there are a couple of basic methods and the variations of personal preferences on those. Neither method is more correct than the other. Use whichever suits you best.

1 Hold the hook between your thumb and index finger much like you would hold a pencil.

2 Alternately, grasp the hook overhand, like you might grasp a knife.

Holding the yarn

Holding the work in your left hand, twine the yarn through the fingers of your left hand. The exact method is not as important as being able to control the yarn well, but try over the index finger, under the middle two and then over the pinkie with the tail coming from the ball.

When you crochet, you will use the section of yarn that runs between the hook and your left index finger. Your index finger will move up and down as you work to create an even tension or tightness in the yarn.

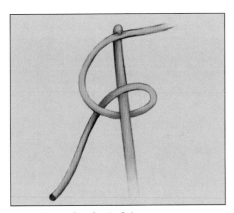

Chain stitch (ch)

1 Make a loop with the long end crossing the short end. Put the hook through the loop and pull the working end through. This slipknot is your first stitch.

2 Yarn over the hook, and draw through the loop. Repeat for the desired number of chain stitches.

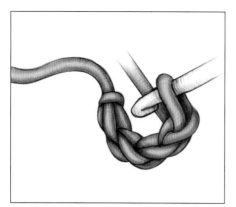

Join to form a ring

1 When your chain is the desired length, use a slip stitch (directions follow) to join it into a ring.

2 Insert the hook into the first chain. Yarn over, and bring yarn through both the stitch and the loop on the hook.

The following basic stitch instructions are for working on a foundation chain.

Slip stitch (sl st)

Insert the hook into the next stitch. Yarn over, and draw the yarn through the stitch and the loop on the hook.

Single crochet (sc)

1 Insert the hook in the second stitch from the hook. Yarn over and draw through the stitch (two loops on the hook).

2 Yarn over and draw through both loops (one loop on the hook).

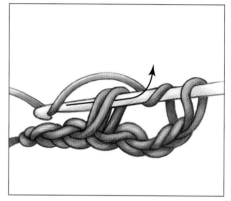

Half-double crochet (hdc)

1 Yarn over. Insert hook through third stitch from hook, yarn over, and draw through stitch (three loops on the hook).

Use up your stash —
Take all your leftover bits and balls of yarn, sort by color, or not, as you choose, and then start knitting and crocheting squares and rectangles. Practice all the stitches you've been wanting to try. When you have enough, sew them together into a pillow cover, set of place mats, a throw for your sofa, or anything else that strikes your fancy.

2 Yarn over and draw through all three loops on the hook (one loop on the hook).

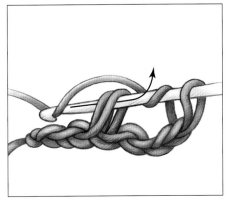

Double crochet (dc)

1 Yarn over. Insert the hook in the fourth stitch from the hook, yarn over, and draw through the stitch (three loops on the hook).

2 Yarn over, draw through two loops on hook (two loops remain on the hook).

3 Yarn over and draw through the remaining two loops on the hook (one loop on the hook).

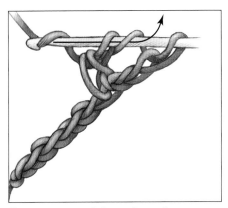

Treble crochet (tr)

1 Yarn over twice. Insert the hook in the fifth stitch from the hook, yarn over, and draw through the stitch (four loops on the hook.)

2 Yarn over and draw through two loops (three loops on the hook).

3 Yarn over and draw through two loops (two loops on the hook).

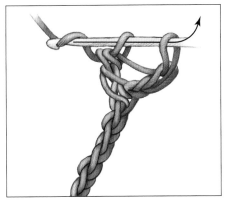

4 Yarn over and draw through both loops (one loop on the hook).

Increasing and decreasing

Increasing and decreasing are simple affairs in crochet. To increase, you work two stitches in the same stitch, thus forming an extra stitch. Unless your pattern instructs otherwise, work the additional stitch in the pattern being worked. Increases may be worked at any point on a row unless you are adding stitches at the beginning or end of a row. In that case, the extra stitches would be added by making a chain with the number of stitches to be added plus enough to turn the row.

Decreases are made by working two stitches together on the last yarn over to decrease one stitch. Several stitches can be decreased at the beginning of a row by working slip stitch across them and beginning the pattern again at the appropriate point. Stitches to be decreased at the end of a row can simply be skipped and the work turned.

Basic symbols used in diagrams

⬯ = Chain

⬬ = Slip stitch

+ = Single crochet

⊤ = Treble

⊤ = Double crochet

⊤ = Half double crochet

FIGURE 1

Pattern Stitch Diagrams

In addition to complete written directions, stitch diagrams for the pattern stitches have been included. If you have never used stitch diagrams before, you may be surprised to find how much of a difference it can make in your enjoyment of a project. For those who prefer visual methods of learning and doing, diagrams can be a boon. Even if you prefer written instructions, diagrams can sometimes clarify a tricky spot. Give them a try and see if they enhance your enjoyment of the craft.

Think of stitch diagrams as "maps" of the crochet fabric. The symbols used approximate the look of the actual stitches they represent. Thus, the diagrams enable you to see what you are going to do before you start and help you keep track of your position as you work. To use them successfully, familiarize yourself with the basic stitches and the symbols that represent them.

From double crochet onward, the number of short angled strokes crossing the stem represents the number of times the yarn is wrapped before the hook is inserted. Diagrams should be read in the same direction as the crochet is worked. Motifs, for example, are worked from the center outward, and all-over patterns are often worked from the bottom to the top. Presented here are the symbols used in this book, with one of the motifs from the cardigan on p. 66 shown as a sample. (See Figures 1 and 2.)

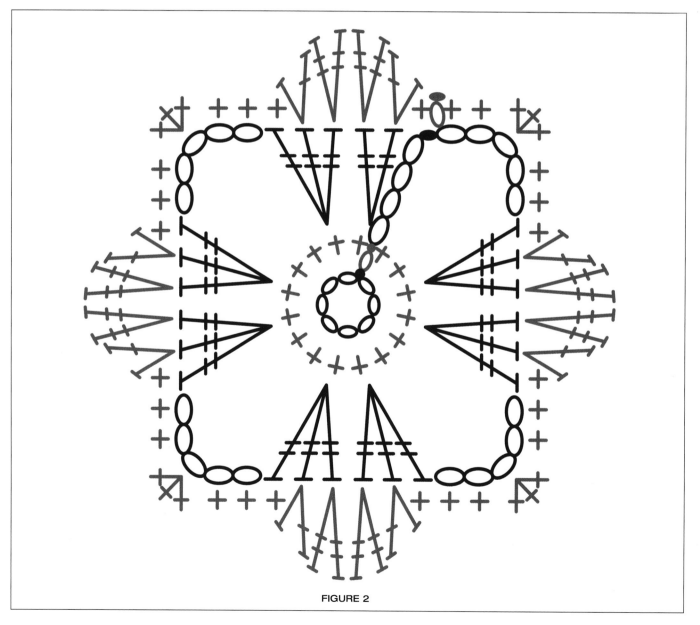

FIGURE 2

FINISHING

Careful finishing is the thing that can make the difference between a project that is exactly what you had in mind and one that you would rather forget about. Sometimes, experienced knitters and crocheters offer finishing services; you can often find out about their services at your local yarn shop or online. However, you should not need to go that far if you take care with the last steps in completing your project. In particular, pay attention to the seams as crooked or puckered seams will not show any project off well.

Use the yarn you worked the pieces with to sew them together. However, if you used a novelty yarn that will be hard to sew with, use a smooth strong yarn in a matching or compatible color. Be sure that the seaming yarn can be cleaned in the same manner as the rest of the project.

As you work, try to keep an even tension on the seam. Pull the yarn snug, but not so tight that the edge or seam puckers. Try to leave a little "give" in the sewing yarn, as this both reduces the chance that it will break and makes a more comfortable seam.

An 18-in. length (45.7cm) of yarn is plenty to sew with. Pulling the yarn repeatedly through the fabric can cause it to break if it is too long.

Here is a good all-purpose seaming stitch, often called "mattress stitch," to get you started. Be sure to keep your seams straight by always inserting your needle in the same place along the seam. This seam is nearly invisible and does not make an unsightly or uncomfortable ridge.

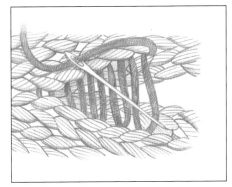

Mattress stitch

Working from the right side, insert yarn needle under the bar between stitches. Then insert the needle under the corresponding bar on the other piece. Continue along the seam for approximately 1 in. (2.5cm), then pull the yarn snug. Repeat until the seam is complete.

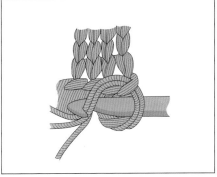

EMBELLISHMENTS
Fringe

Simple fringe is made by cutting yarn twice the desired length with extra for knotting. Fold the yarn in half over a crochet hook. From the wrong side of the work, insert hook from front to back through work. Pull yarn ends through work and loop and tighten.

Finish all fringe before trimming to the desired length.

Blocking is the process of wetting, pressing, or steaming garment pieces to set their permanent size and shape. Wool responds best to this process; blocking might not be as successful or necessary with fibers other than wool.

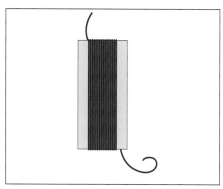

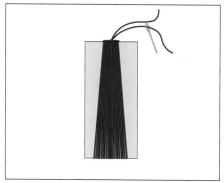

Tassels

1 Cut a piece of cardboard 2 in. (5cm) wide and as long as you want the tassel. Wrap the yarn around the cardboard lengthwise. The more wraps, the more generous your tassel will be.

2 Use a yarn needle to thread a length of yarn under the wrapped yarn, at the edge of the cardboard. Pull tightly and tie firmly. This is the top of your tassel.

3 Cut yarn at opposite end from tie. Remove cardboard.

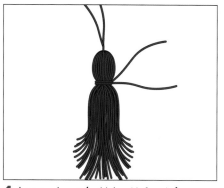

4 Approximately ½ in. (1.3cm) from top of tassel, firmly tie another length of yarn around the "neck" of the tassel. Wrap the yarn a few times if you like. Trim bottom of tassel evenly.

Be sure to purchase enough yarn to finish your project. If at all possible, buy an extra skein just in case. Extra yarn is always handy to have around, especially for embellishments!

I-cords

Knitting lore has it that the "I" in I-cord stands for "Idiot" because the cord is considered so easy to make. Perhaps a more pleasant way to refer to it would be "Intelligent" cord. An I-cord, usually made on double-pointed needles, can also be worked on a knitting spool, also called a knitting knobby.

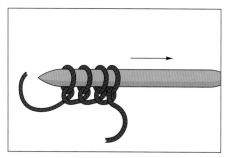

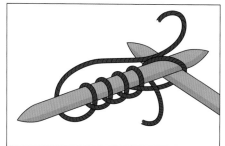

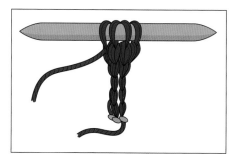

Knitting an I-cord

1 Cast on three to five stitches. Knit one row. Without turning the work, slide the stitches back to the other end of the needle.

2 Pull the yarn tightly from the bottom to the top and knit across.

3 Repeat steps 1–2 until your I-cord is the desired length. Cut yarn and thread end through stitches to secure.

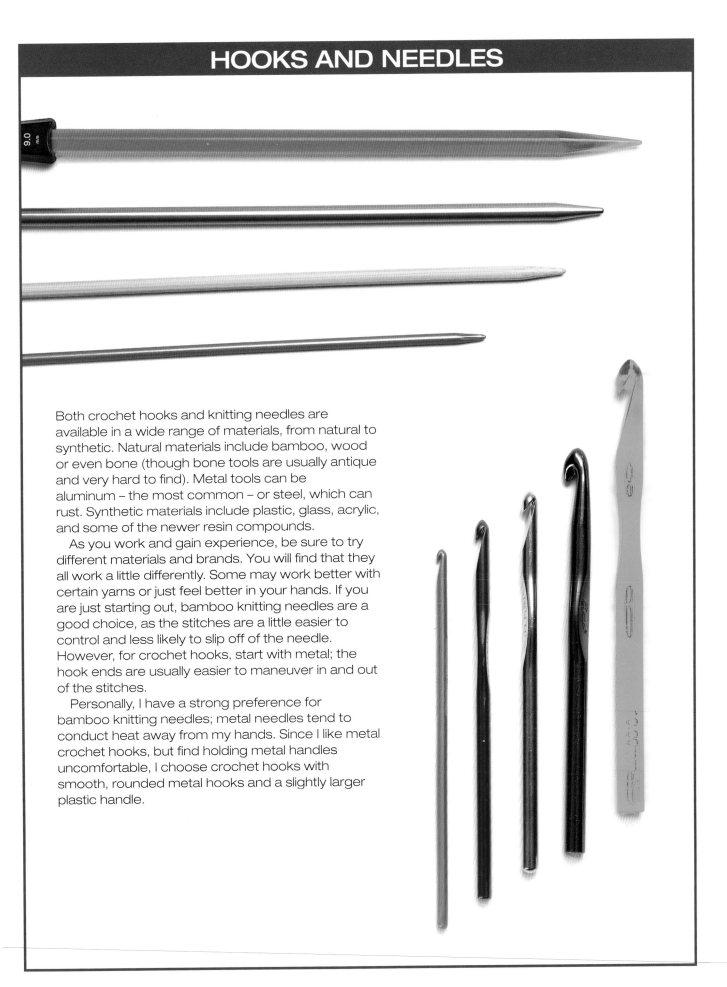

Both crochet hooks and knitting needles are available in a wide range of materials, from natural to synthetic. Natural materials include bamboo, wood or even bone (though bone tools are usually antique and very hard to find). Metal tools can be aluminum – the most common – or steel, which can rust. Synthetic materials include plastic, glass, acrylic, and some of the newer resin compounds.

As you work and gain experience, be sure to try different materials and brands. You will find that they all work a little differently. Some may work better with certain yarns or just feel better in your hands. If you are just starting out, bamboo knitting needles are a good choice, as the stitches are a little easier to control and less likely to slip off of the needle. However, for crochet hooks, start with metal; the hook ends are usually easier to maneuver in and out of the stitches.

Personally, I have a strong preference for bamboo knitting needles; metal needles tend to conduct heat away from my hands. Since I like metal crochet hooks, but find holding metal handles uncomfortable, I choose crochet hooks with smooth, rounded metal hooks and a slightly larger plastic handle.

PORTABLE PROJECTS

Knit and crochet projects are quite portable, and I like to make transporting them even easier. I keep several small plastic lidded boxes, each containing the tools I find essential. (Sometimes I need to add specialty items, such as cable needles, but for the most part, these boxes contain everything I need to make and finish a project.) I always have several of these "kits" ready, so I can add my project and go.

I use boxes that measure approximately 5 x 3 in. (13 x 7.6cm); they're available at craft and discount stores. My boxes include:

- small sharp scissors for cutting yarn and thread
- a good quality measuring tape, retractable or not as you prefer
- stitch markers of some type. I actually have a mix in each box of plain ring markers and split ring markers
- a couple of small stitch holders
- one or two yarn or tapestry needles
- long, heavy pins with large plastic heads for pinning pieces together
- a set of point protectors

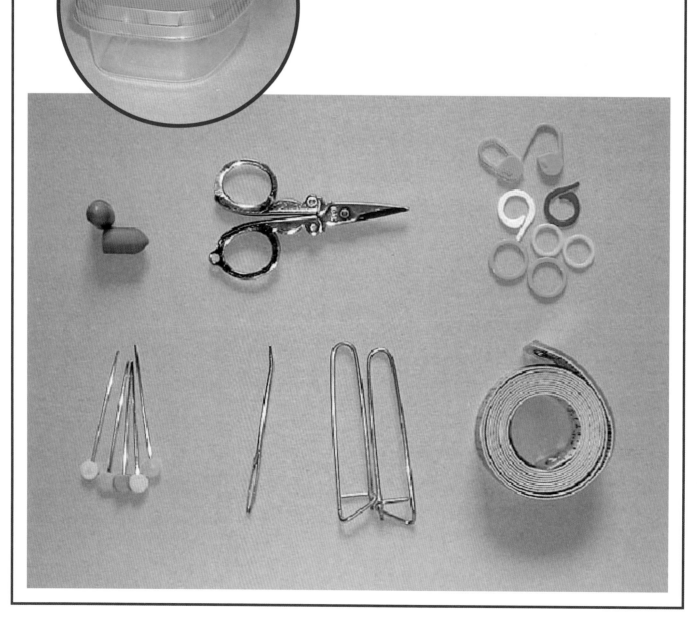

Resources

Useful – and just plain cool – knit and crochet books and Web sites

Books

Bead & Felted Tapestry Crochet, by Carol Ventura
Teaches how to combine tapestry crochet with beads, how to felt your crochet, and how to felt with beads.

The Crochet Answer Book: Solutions to Every Problem You'll Ever Face; Answers to Every Question You'll Ever Ask, by Edie Eckman
The title says it all.

How to Knit, by Debbie Bliss
Presented as a series of workshops to move forward from beginning projects.

The "I Hate to Finish Sweaters" Guide to Finishing Sweaters, by Janet Szabo
A comprehensive guide to finishing.

Knitting from the Top, by Barbara G. Walker
How to knit nearly any garment – sweaters, skirts, pants, and more – from the top down.

Knitting Without Tears, by Elizabeth Zimmermann
A knitting classic. Well worth reading for knitters of all ages and skill levels.

The New Crochet: 40 Wonderful Wearables, by Terry Taylor
Stylish, contemporary patterns from a variety of artists that use familiar and easy-to-learn stitches.

Stitch 'N Bitch: The Knitter's Handbook, by Debbie Stoller
A new knitting classic for young and young-at-heart knitters.

Stitch 'N Bitch Crochet: The Happy Hooker, by Debbie Stoller
On its way to becoming a reference standard for new needleworkers.

Vogue Knitting: The Ultimate Knitting Book, from the editors of *Vogue Knitting* magazine
A comprehensive basic reference book.

Web sites

buttons.com
The Web site of manufacturer JHB International: buttons, findings, and more.

crafster.org
A forum for all types of craft and handwork. The place to ask specific questions.

crochet.org
The Crochet Guild of America is dedicated to preserving and advancing the art of crochet.

crochetinsider.com
Webzine to find news about developments in the industry, exchange ideas, and read designer interviews.

crochetme.com
A webzine for contemporary, cool, hip, fashionable crochet.

crochetpartners.org
A world-wide group of crocheters who enjoys sharing information, tips, and experiences.

interweave.com
Web home of *Interweave Knits* and *Interweave Crochet*, the magazines for elegant knit and crochet.

knittinghelp.com
More than 150 free videos help you learn to knit or brush up on techniques.

knitty.com
Free webzine with a sense of humor.

lionbrand.com
The Web site of Lion Brand Yarn Company. View a full line of yarns, dozens of free patterns, and helpful tips.

patternworks.com
Request free full-color catalog that's a treat in the mailbox. It bills itself as "everything for the hand knitter and crocheter."

schoolhousepress.com
A great resource for solid needlework education and some wonderful, hard-to-find yarns.

shinydesigns.com
Find information and patterns for knitting, crochet, and other types of needlework.

vogueknitting.com
Find fashion-forward style ranging from simple to expert levels.

wiseneedle.com
Yarn reviews, information, and advice.

yarnstandards.com
Sponsored by the Craft Yarn Council of America, this site collects standard guidelines on yarn weights, pattern levels, pattern sizing, and more.

yarndex.com
Find information on yarns such as weight, yardage, price, colors, and user reviews.

Acknowledgments

A multitude of people played roles, both large and small, in the completion of this book. My thanks go to all who helped me in any way, and special thanks go to:

A wonderful team of editors: Kristin Schneidler, who truly got this project started, Pat Lantier, who kept it on track and answered my many questions at critical points, and Karin Buckingham who stepped in for the finish.

Mim Holden, the absolutely lovely lady who made the majority of the sample projects in the book. She is a joy to work with, and I am certain I could never have finished everything in time without her.

My husband, whose matter-of-fact attitude toward this undertaking (and many others) makes anything seem possible. Thank you for your steadfast belief in my ability and your loving support of my work.

Carolyn Hawkins, a true Renaissance woman, for proofreading critical parts and sharing her own limitless creativity.

Denise Miller, for proofing and testing most of the crochet patterns. Thank you for seeing what I could no longer see.

My mother, for her interest in the book and her delight in seeing my name in print.

Lion Brand Yarn Company, for graciously and generously providing the yarns and helping make the projects a success.

JHB International, who generously provided the buttons and closures that give that last bit of polish.

Monette Lassiter Satterfield, an artist and freelance designer for the arts and crafts industry, learned to embroider and crochet as a young girl. Learning to knit came later, but she took to it with great enthusiasm. Monette is a native Floridian without much call for heavy sweaters, but she still takes great pleasure in designing knit and crochet projects. Visit her Web site at shinydesigns.com.